The Bucks Begin Here

The Bucks Begin Here

A Financial Guide

John V. Medeiros

iUniverse, Inc.
New York Lincoln Shanghai

The Bucks Begin Here
A Financial Guide

iUniverse, Inc.

For information address:
iUniverse
2021 Pine Lake Road, Suite 100
Lincoln, NE 68512
www.iuniverse.com

ISBN: 0-595-27942-2

Printed in the United States of America

Contents

About The Author

John V. Medeiros has an extensive background in real estate appraisals and sales, finance, taxes, banking, and life and health insurance, including Medicare supplements and Long Term Care Coverage.

Background

- Deputy Chief Appraiser of the U.S. Department of Housing and Urban Development (FHA), (14 years of service)
- Served as an appraiser-consultant in the tax department for the Commonwealth of Massachusetts (1967–1971).
- Served as treasurer-manager of a federal credit union for 21 years and as president of the William J. Cyr Chapter of Federal Credit Unions.
- Vice-president of the AACA (American Association of Certified Appraisers, Chapter 1, Southeastern Massachusetts (1991–1995).
- Licensed in Massachusetts and Rhode Island as a certified residential appraiser (CRA).
- Consultant for: nursing homes, multifamily housing, residential, commercial, and industrial evaluations.
- Certified Review Appraiser-NA-RA/MU (National Association of Review Appraisers and Mortgage Underwriters).
- Licensed in Massachusetts and Rhode Island as a broker in real estate appraisals and sales.
- Licensed general agent in Massachusetts and Rhode Island in life and health insurance.
- Notary public for many years, still serving.

Education

- U.S. Army Air Force 1942-1945; 1st Lieutenant, Navigator
- Air-to-ground Liaison Observer, Intelligence Officer and Briefing Officer
- Received 5 medals for service in all four corners of the world

- Over 700 hours of flying time
- Attended and graduated from Air-Navigation Schools in 1942
- 1978 Graduate of Roger Williams College (magna cum laude) with B.S.A. degree in Public Administration
- Attended many schools dealing with advanced accounting, taxes, real estate, appraising, life and health insurance-
- Since retirement from government service in 1985 has been self employed, performing over one thousand real estate appraisals

The Bucks Begin Here

A Financial Guide for the Financially Uninformed!

Introduction

What you don't know can hurt you!

This publication is sold with the understanding that the author is not engaged in rendering accounting, legal or other professional service. Although the book intends to provide accurate, valuable information, the services of a competent professional should be sought if legal advice or other expert assistance is required.

This book should enable you to save hundreds to many thousands of dollars, with step by step methods that will show you:

- How to know what income producing properties are worth, from possible purchases of small to large businesses, apartment houses, and all other income producing properties
- How to value 2 to 4 family residences
- How to save many thousands of dollars on your mortgage payments (with the same monthly payment) by using various methods
- When refinancing is advisable and when it is not
- Wise ways to approach the purchase of a single family residence
- What you should know about condominiums and cooperatives (Co-ops), with good sound advice and information about possible pitfalls
- What you should know about H.U.D./F.H.A. and V.A. loans, along with information concerning their eligibility and desirability
- Where to go and what to do for conventional financing

- Building terms and illustrations
- How to find out if you are overpaying your real estate taxes and what you can do about it

This book is designed to help the financially uninformed by describing the many ways available to save or earn lots of money.

The Bucks Begin Here

This book could save you hundreds to thousands of dollars on purchases of income producing properties.

Step by step methods of estimating the value of income producing properties are illustrated in easy to follow formulas and explanations.

Although the use of this book will help you estimate, beforehand, what a particular property is worth and save you countless hours and expense, it is not intended to be a substitute for an appraisal by a certified, licensed appraiser. A licensed appraisal will verify the estimated property value plus all the requirements involved in the appraisal such as zoning, etc., in order to be able to obtain a bank loan, if desired. The use of this book will enable you to decide whether or not to follow through with the purchase of income property, saving the cost of the appraisal and possible bank charges. This book will enable you to make estimates to help you to decide whether the purchase of a particular income property's projected net income will support the return to equity and loan payments.

The formulas shown below are for income producing properties only, with the value determined by the income method of valuation, where income refers to net income, which is gross income minus expenses,

The value of the land, building, goodwill, etc. are all combined for one total value, which is that value produced by the income method of valuation as shown, in the following illustrations and examples.

Gross income is the income produced from all sources. Expenses are those created by the property.

Net income is the result of the expenses subtracted from the gross income.

Gross income is the estimated income derived at 100 % occupancy in the cases of rental property. However, as full occupancy is rarely obtained, the usual ratios applied to the gross income are:

97% for elderly apartments
95% for family apartments
90% for commercial occupancy

The history of the property in question will give the best ratio to be utilized. The determination of the correct net income affects the correct valuation.

If the profit and loss statement can be obtained from the property's federal tax return, the net income shown in the profit and loss statement will give a good indication of the present value of the property, by means of the formula shown below.

Expected gross income	$100,000
Multiplied by estimated occupancy ratio	x 95%
Equals effective gross income	$95,000
Minus estimated expenses-	-$30,000
Equals net income	$65,000

The net income stream is the key to the valuation.

The following interest table is utilized to obtain a debt service rate.

Conventional Loan Payment Factors For Monthly Payments Per $1,000

Years	6	6.25	6.5	6.75	7	7.25	7.5	7.75	8
1	86.0664	86.1814	86.2964	86.4115	86.5267	86.6420	86.7574	86.8729	86.9884
2	44.3206	44.4333	44.5463	44.6593	44.7726	44.8860	44.9996	45.1134	45.2273
3	30.4219	30.5353	30.6490	30.7629	30.8771	30.9915	31.1062	31.2212	31.3364
4	23.4850	23.5998	23.7150	23.8304	23.9462	24.0624	24.1789	24.2957	24.4129
5	19.3328	19.4493	19.5661	19.6835	19.8012	19.9194	20.0379	20.1570	20.2764
6	16.5729	16.6912	16.8099	16.9292	17.0490	17.1693	17.2901	17.4114	17.5332
7	14.6086	14.7287	14.8494	14.9708	15.0927	15.2152	15.3383	15.4620	15.5862
8	13.1414	13.2635	13.3862	13.5096	13.6337	13.7585	13.8839	14.0099	14.1367
9	12.0057	12.1298	12.2545	12.3800	12.5063	12.6333	12.7610	12.8895	13.0187
10	11.1021	11.2280	11.3548	11.4824	11.6108	11.7401	11.8702	12.0011	12.1328
11	10.3670	10.4949	10.6238	10.7535	10.8841	11.0156	11.1480	11.2813	11.4154
12	9.7585	9.8884	10.0192	10.1510	10.2838	10.4176	10.5523	10.6879	10.8245

13	9.2472	9.3790	9.5119	9.6458	9.7807	9.9167	10.0537	10.1917	10.3307
14	8.8124	8.9461	9.0810	9.2169	9.3540	9.4922	9.6314	9.7718	9.9132
15	8.4386	8.5742	8.7111	8.8491	8.9883	9.1286	9.2701	9.4128	9.5565
16	8.1144	8.2519	8.3908	8.5308	8.6721	8.8146	8.9583	9.1032	9.2493
17	7.8310	7.9705	8.1112	8.2533	8.3966	8.5412	8.6871	8.8342	8.9826
18	7.5816	7.7229	7.8656	8.0096	8.1550	8.3017	8.4497	8.5990	8.7496
19	7.3608	7.5040	7.6486	7.7945	7.9419	8.0907	8.2408	8.3922	8.5450
20	7.1643	7.3093	7.4557	7.6036	7.7530	7.9038	8.0559	8.2095	8.3644
21	6.9886	7.1353	7.2836	7.4334	7.5847	7.7375	7.8917	8.0473	8.2043
22	6.8307	6.9793	7.1294	7.2811	7.4342	7.5889	7.7451	7.9027	8.0618
23	6.6885	6.8387	6.9906	7.1441	7.2992	7.4558	7.6139	7.7735	7.9345
24	6.5598	6.7118	6.8654	7.0207	7.1776	7.3361	7.4960	7.6576	7.8205
25	6.4430	6.5967	6.7521	6.9091	7.0678	7.2281	7.3899	7.5533	7.7182
26	6.3368	6.4921	6.6492	6.8079	6.9684	7.1304	7.2941	7.4593	7.6260
27	6.2399	6.3968	6.5555	6.7160	6.8781	7.0419	7.2073	7.3743	7.5428
28	6.1512	6.3098	6.4702	6.6323	6.7961	6.9616	7.1287	7.2974	7.4676
29	6.0700	6.2302	6.3921	6.5558	6.7213	6.8884	7.0572	7.2276	7.3995
30	5.9955	6.1572	6.3207	6.4860	6.6530	6.8218	6.9921	7.1641	7.3376
31	5.9269	6.0901	6.2552	6.4220	6.5906	6.7609	6.9328	7.1064	7.2815
32	5.8638	6.0284	6.1950	6.3633	6.5334	6.7052	6.8787	7.0538	7.2304
33	5.8055	5.9716	6.1396	6.3094	6.4810	6.6543	6.8292	7.0057	7.1838
34	5.7517	5.9192	6.0886	6.2598	6.4328	6.6075	6.7839	6.9619	7.1414

A debt service rate refers to the payment of principal and interest on a loan. This debt service rate is applied to the net income as shown in the following examples:

Subject property net income	$12,010

Cash flow rate
(desired rate of return on the investment, or down payment) 10.2%

Best available mortgage financing for property:

Loan value ratio	90%
Interest rate	6.75%
Initial curtail (factor to pay the principal)	1.50%

(interest rate and initial curtail combined are the yearly payments to the bank, or monthly payment times 12 months for yearly payment)

Mortgage insurance premium (MIP), if any	0.50%

Debt service rate equals
Interest rate+Initial curtail+MIP   6.75+1.50+0.50=8.75%

Example: 90% mortgage term from the bank plus investor's 10% equity (down payment) equals 100%.

The rate of cash flow to equity (investor' own payment) can be used to develop an overall capitalization rate, as follows:

Debt service rate of 8.75% x 90% obtainable mortgage=   7.875%
Cash flow to equity rate 10.2% x 10% equity=   +1.020%
Overall rate by cash flow method=   8.895%

Net income $12,010 divided by 8.895% rate=$135,000 Capitalized Value (12,010/0.0895=135,000)

The next six pages will further illustrate the concept of debt service rate.

Another example using the following Mortgage Factor table:

Conventional Loan Payment Factors For Monthly Payments Per $1,000

Rate Years	7	7.25	7.5	7.75	8	8.25	8.5	8.75	9
1	86.5267	86.6420	86.7574	86.8729	86.9884	87.1041	87.2198	87.3356	87.4515
2	44.7726	44.8860	44.9996	45.1134	45.2273	45.3414	45.4557	45.5701	45.6847
3	30.8771	30.9915	31.1062	31.2212	31.3364	31.4518	31.5675	31.6835	31.7997
4	23.9462	24.0624	24.1789	24.2957	24.4129	24.5304	24.6483	24.7665	24.8850
5	19.8012	19.9194	20.0379	20.1570	20.2764	20.3963	20.5165	20.6372	20.7584
6	17.0490	17.1693	17.2901	17.4114	17.5332	17.6556	17.7784	17.9017	18.0255
7	15.0927	15.2152	15.3383	15.4620	15.5862	15.7111	15.8365	15.9625	16.0891
8	13.6337	13.7585	13.8839	14.0099	14.1367	14.2641	14.3921	14.5208	14.6502
9	12.5063	12.6333	12.7610	12.8895	13.0187	13.1487	13.2794	13.4108	13.5429
10	11.6108	11.7401	11.8702	12.0011	12.1328	12.2653	12.3986	12.5327	12.6676
11	10.8841	11.0156	11.1480	11.2813	11.4154	11.5505	11.6864	11.8232	11.9608
12	10.2838	10.4176	10.5523	10.6879	10.8245	10.9621	11.1006	11.2400	11.3803
13	9.7807	9.9167	10.0537	10.1917	10.3307	10.4708	10.6118	10.7538	10.8968
14	9.3540	9.4922	9.6314	9.7718	9.9132	10.0557	10.1992	10.3438	10.4894
15	8.9883	9.1286	9.2701	9.4128	9.5565	9.7014	9.8474	9.9945	10.1427
16	8.6721	8.8146	8.9583	9.1032	9.2493	9.3965	9.5449	9.6945	9.8452
17	8.3966	8.5412	8.6871	8.8342	8.9826	9.1321	9.2829	9.4349	9.5880
18	8.1550	8.3017	8.4497	8.5990	8.7496	8.9015	9.0546	9.2089	9.3644
19	7.9419	8.0907	8.2408	8.3922	8.5450	8.6991	8.8545	9.0111	9.1690
20	7.7530	7.9038	8.0559	8.2095	8.3644	8.5207	8.6782	8.8371	8.9973
21	7.5847	7.7375	7.8917	8.0473	8.2043	8.3627	8.5224	8.6834	8.8458
22	7.4342	7.5889	7.7451	7.9027	8.0618	8.2222	8.3841	8.5472	8.7117
23	7.2992	7.4558	7.6139	7.7735	7.9345	8.0970	8.2609	8.4261	8.5927
24	7.1776	7.3361	7.4960	7.6576	7.8205	7.9850	8.1508	8.3181	8.4866
25	7.0678	7.2281	7.3899	7.5533	7.7182	7.8845	8.0523	8.2214	8.3920
26	6.9684	7.1304	7.2941	7.4593	7.6260	7.7942	7.9638	8.1348	8.3072
27	6.8781	7.0419	7.2073	7.3743	7.5428	7.7128	7.8842	8.0570	8.2313
28	6.7961	6.9616	7.1287	7.2974	7.4676	7.6393	7.8125	7.9871	8.1630
29	6.7213	6.8884	7.0572	7.2276	7.3995	7.5729	7.7477	7.9240	8.1016
30	6.6530	6.8218	6.9921	7.1641	7.3376	7.5127	7.6891	7.8670	8.0462

30-year term, equal payments monthly per $1000, interest rate of 7.3376%, which can be rounded to 7.34%

7.34% x 12 months=88.08

88.08 divided by 1000=0.08808=8.808% debt service rate without MIP

Add 0.5 to include MIP or 8.808+0.5=9.308% debt service rate

Another example using the following Mortgage Factor table:

Conventional Loan Payment Factors For Monthly Payments Per $1,000

Years	6.5	6.6	6.7	6.8	6.9	7	7.1	7.2	7.3
11	10.6238	10.6755	10.7275	10.7795	10.8317	10.8841	10.9366	10.9892	11.0420
12	10.0192	10.0718	10.1246	10.1775	10.2306	10.2838	10.3372	10.3907	10.4444
13	9.5119	9.5653	9.6189	9.6727	9.7266	9.7807	9.8350	9.8894	9.9440
14	9.0810	9.1352	9.1896	9.2443	9.2990	9.3540	9.4091	9.4645	9.5199
15	8.7111	8.7661	8.8214	8.8768	8.9325	8.9883	9.0443	9.1005	9.1568
16	8.3908	8.4466	8.5027	8.5590	8.6154	8.6721	8.7289	8.7860	8.8432
17	8.1112	8.1679	8.2248	8.2818	8.3391	8.3966	8.4543	8.5122	8.5703
18	7.8656	7.9231	7.9807	8.0386	8.0967	8.1550	8.2135	8.2723	8.3312
19	7.6486	7.7068	7.7652	7.8239	7.8828	7.9419	8.0013	8.0608	8.1206
20	7.4557	7.5147	7.5739	7.6334	7.6931	7.7530	7.8131	7.8735	7.9341
21	7.2836	7.3434	7.4034	7.4636	7.5240	7.5847	7.6456	7.7068	7.7682
22	7.1294	7.1899	7.2506	7.3116	7.3728	7.4342	7.4959	7.5579	7.6201
23	6.9906	7.0519	7.1133	7.1750	7.2370	7.2992	7.3616	7.4243	7.4873
24	6.8654	6.9273	6.9895	7.0520	7.1147	7.1776	7.2408	7.3042	7.3679
25	6.7521	6.8147	6.8776	6.9407	7.0041	7.0678	7.1318	7.1959	7.2603

Interest rate of 7.1% for 25 years
Monthly payment per $1000=7.1318 x 12 months=85.5816
85.5816 divided by 1000=0.0855816 or 8.55816% debt service rate.

Lets say that conventional loans can be obtained at that rate, with 80%-financing, with 20% down, and the desired return to equity is 10%, or 10% desired return on the investment, then:

Debt service rate=8.55816 x 80% (0.80)=   6.846528
Desired equity return=10.00 x 20% (0.20)=   +2.000000
Capitalization rate=   8.846528

If the net income from the property is $80,000 then $80,000 divided by the capitalization rate of 0.8846528=$904,310 estimated fair market value

Proof:

Estimated value of $904,310 x 80% mortgage= $723,448 financing by bank
Equity investment of 20% of $904,310= $180,862 down payment
Total= $904,310 value of property

$904,310 x debt service rate of 6.846528%= $61,913.77
$904,310 x equity return of 2.00%=   +$18,086.20
Net income= $79,999.97

This is close enough to the property's net income of $80,000

Another example using the following table illustrating the monthly payment to principal and interest rate per $1,000

Interest Rate	Maximum Term in Years	Maximum Term in Months	Number of Payments	Initial Curtail Rates	Monthly Payment to Principal and Interest Rate per $1,000*
6 ¾ %	40	0	480	0.490282 %	$6.033568
6 ¾	35	0	420	0.706998	6.214165
6 ¾	30	0	360	1.033177	6.485981
6 ¾	25	0	300	1.540938	6.909115
6 ¾	20	0	240	2.374368	7.603640
6 ¾	15	0	180	3.868914	8.849095
6 ¾	10	0	120	7.028893	11.482411

*The monthly payment for a loan on the Level Annuity Monthly Payment basis is calculated by dividing the mortgage amount by 1,000, multiplying the result by the applied figure in the Monthly Payment. to Principal column and rounding to the next higher whole cent.

To obtain debt service rate (the rate required to service the mortgage) you add the interest rate plus the initial curtail.

Assuming interest rate of 6 ¾% (6.75) for a 40 year term and a payment to principal factor (initial curtail) of 0.490282:

Interest rate: 6.75
Initial curtail: +0.490282
Debt service rate: 7.24028%

Another way to obtain the debt service rate:

See monthly payment to principal and interest rate per $1000 in the above table.

At 6 ¾% this would be $6.033568

You then multiply by 12 months: 6.033568 x 12=72.4028

And then divide this by 1000: 72.4028/1000=0.0724028 or 7.24028% debt service rate

Again, the debt service rate or the rate necessary to service the mortgage when added to the rate of equity return (which is the desired return to the investor) results in a capitalization rate.

When the estimated net income is divided by the capitalization rate the resultant is called the capitalized value, or the estimated value of the property.

Another example using the following Mortgage Factor table:

Conventional Loan Payment Factors For Monthly Payments Per $1,000

Years	Rate 9	9.25	9.5	9.75	10	10.25	10.5	10.75	11
16	9.8452	9.9970	10.1499	10.3039	10.4590	10.6152	10.7724	10.9307	11.0900
17	9.5880	9.7423	9.8978	10.0544	10.2121	10.3709	10.5308	10.6918	10.8538
18	9.3644	9.5212	9.6791	9.8382	9.9984	10.1598	10.3223	10.4858	10.6505
19	9.1690	9.3281	9.4884	9.6499	9.8126	9.9764	10.1414	10.3075	10.4746
20	8.9973	9.1587	9.3213	9.4852	9.6502	9.8164	9.9838	10.1523	10.3219
21	8.8458	9.0094	9.1743	9.3405	9.5078	9.6763	9.8460	10.0168	10.1887
22	8.7117	8.8775	9.0446	9.2129	9.3825	9.5532	9.7251	9.8981	10.0722
23	8.5927	8.7606	8.9297	9.1002	9.2718	9.4447	9.6187	9.7938	9.9701
24	8.4866	8.6566	8.8277	9.0002	9.1739	9.3488	9.5248	9.7020	9.8803
25	8.3920	8.5638	8.7370	8.9114	9.0870	9.2638	9.4418	9.6209	9.8011
26	8.3072	8.4810	8.6560	8.8323	9.0098	9.1885	9.3683	9.5492	9.7313
27	8.2313	8.4068	8.5836	8.7617	8.9410	9.1214	9.3030	9.4857	9.6695
28	8.1630	8.3403	8.5188	8.6986	8.8796	9.0618	9.2450	9.4294	9.6148
29	8.1016	8.2805	8.4607	8.6421	8.8248	9.0085	9.1934	9.3793	9.5663
30	8.0462	8.2268	8.4085	8.5915	8.7758	8.9610	9.1474	9.3348	9.5232

Assume an interest rate of 10% for 30 years.
Monthly payment per $1000=8.7758 x 12 months=105.3096
You then divide by 1000: 105.3096/1000=0.1053096 or 10.53096% debt service rate.

Assuming net income of $60,000,with desired equity return of 15%:

Utilizing formula with 75% financing and 25% down payment:

Debt service rate 10.53096 x 75% (0.75) financing=	7.89822
Desired equity return 15 x 25% (0.25) down payment=	+3.75
Capitalization rate=	11.64822

With assumed net income at $60,000 then 60,000 divided by capitalization rate of 11.64822%=515,100.16

$60,000/0.1164822=$515,100 capitalized value
This capitalized value is also called the fair market value of the property.

Proof:

Estimated value of $515,100 x debt service rate of 0.0789822=	$40,683.73
Estimated value of $515,100 x equity return of 0.0375=	+$19,316.25
This results in a close enough net income of	$59,999.98
and	
estimated value of $515,100 x 75% mortgage=	$386,325.00 amount of loan
equity investment of 25% x $515,100=	+$128,775.00 down payment
Estimated capitalized value=	$515,100.00 fair market value
	of the property

Summary For Income Producing Properties

To have monetary value, a property must generate income. The property expenses reduce the gross income, which is the income from all sources, the result is called net income.

The net income must support the desired mortgage.

Utilizing the interest tables, the following known facts are available:

Factors for monthly payment per $1000 derived from number of years at various interest rates.

Conventional Loan Payment Factors For Monthly Payments Per $1,000

	Rate								
Years	7	7.25	7.5	7.75	8	8.25	8.5	8.75	9
21	7.5847	7.7375	7.8917	8.0473	8.2043	8.3627	8.5224	8.6834	8.8458
22	7.4342	7.5889	7.7451	7.9027	8.0618	8.2222	8.3841	8.5472	8.7117
23	7.2992	7.4558	7.6139	7.7735	7.9345	8.0970	8.2609	8.4261	8.5927
24	7.1776	7.3361	7.4960	7.6576	7.8205	7.9850	8.1508	8.3181	8.4866
25	7.0678	7.2281	7.3899	7.5533	7.7182	7.8845	8.0523	8.2214	8.3920
26	6.9684	7.1304	7.2941	7.4593	7.6260	7.7942	7.9638	8.1348	8.3072
27	6.8781	7.0419	7.2073	7.3743	7.5428	7.7128	7.8842	8.0570	8.2313
28	6.7961	6.9616	7.1287	7.2974	7.4676	7.6393	7.8125	7.9871	8.1630
29	6.7213	6.8884	7.0572	7.2276	7.3995	7.5729	7.7477	7.9240	8.1016
30	6.6530	6.8218	6.9921	7.1641	7.3376	7.5127	7.6891	7.8670	8.0462

This table shows conventional loan payment factors for monthly payment per $1000.

Utilizing the table you will see next to 30 years the figure 7.3377 which is the monthly payment to the interest figure at 8% for a 30-year period. As the net income is estimated for a yearly basis, you multiply the 7.3377, or 7.34 by 12 (12 months) for 7.34 x 12=88.08, then divide by 1000 or 88.08/1000=0.08808 or 8.0808% debt service rate.

Let us say that conventional loans can be obtained at that rate, with 80% financing and 20% down and the investor, you, expect a return on your down payment of 10%, then:

Debt service rate=	8.0808 x 80%=	6.46464
Desired equity return on your investment=	10.00 x. 20%=	2.00
Capitalization rate=		8.46464

If the net income from the property is $85,000, then $85,000 divided by the capitalization rate of 8.46464% (0.0846464)=$1,0041177.30 capitalized value.

Proof:
Capitalized value at 80% financing (loan amount)
=$1,004,177 x 80%= $803,341.60
Capitalized value at 20% down payment
=$1,004,177 x 20%= $200,835.40
Total value of property= $1,004,177.00

Capitalization Rates

Once again, the following interest table is utilized to obtain a debt service rate.

Conventional Loan Payment Factors For Monthly Payments Per $1,000

Years	Rate 6	6.25	6.5	6.75	7	7.25	7.5	7.75	8
1	86.0664	86.1814	86.2964	86.4115	86.5267	86.6420	86.7574	86.8729	86.9884
2	44.3206	44.4333	44.5463	44.6593	44.7726	44.8860	44.9996	45.1134	45.2273
3	30.4219	30.5353	30.6490	30.7629	30.8771	30.9915	31.1062	31.2212	31.3364
4	23.4850	23.5998	23.7150	23.8304	23.9462	24.0624	24.1789	24.2957	24.4129
5	19.3328	19.4493	19.5661	19.6835	19.8012	19.9194	20.0379	20.1570	20.2764
6	16.5729	16.6912	16.8099	16.9292	17.0490	17.1693	17.2901	17.4114	17.5332
7	14.6086	14.7287	14.8494	14.9708	15.0927	15.2152	15.3383	15.4620	15.5862
8	13.1414	13.2635	13.3862	13.5096	13.6337	13.7585	13.8839	14.0099	14.1367
9	12.0057	12.1298	12.2545	12.3800	12.5063	12.6333	12.7610	12.8895	13.0187
10	11.1021	11.2280	11.3548	11.4824	11.6108	11.7401	11.8702	12.0011	12.1328
11	10.3670	10.4949	10.6238	10.7535	10.8841	11.0156	11.1480	11.2813	11.4154
12	9.7585	9.8884	10.0192	10.1510	10.2838	10.4176	10.5523	10.6879	10.8245
13	9.2472	9.3790	9.5119	9.6458	9.7807	9.9167	10.0537	10.1917	10.3307
14	8.8124	8.9461	9.0810	9.2169	9.3540	9.4922	9.6314	9.7718	9.9132
15	8.4386	8.5742	8.7111	8.8491	8.9883	9.1286	9.2701	9.4128	9.5565
16	8.1144	8.2519	8.3908	8.5308	8.6721	8.8146	8.9583	9.1032	9.2493
17	7.8310	7.9705	8.1112	8.2533	8.3966	8.5412	8.6871	8.8342	8.9826
18	7.5816	7.7229	7.8656	8.0096	8.1550	8.3017	8.4497	8.5990	8.7496
19	7.3608	7.5040	7.6486	7.7945	7.9419	8.0907	8.2408	8.3922	8.5450
20	7.1643	7.3093	7.4557	7.6036	7.7530	7.9038	8.0559	8.2095	8.3644
21	6.9886	7.1353	7.2836	7.4334	7.5847	7.7375	7.8917	8.0473	8.2043
22	6.8307	6.9793	7.1294	7.2811	7.4342	7.5889	7.7451	7.9027	8.0618
23	6.6885	6.8387	6.9906	7.1441	7.2992	7.4558	7.6139	7.7735	7.9345
24	6.5598	6.7118	6.8654	7.0207	7.1776	7.3361	7.4960	7.6576	7.8205
25	6.4430	6.5967	6.7521	6.9091	7.0678	7.2281	7.3899	7.5533	7.7182
26	6.3368	6.4921	6.6492	6.8079	6.9684	7.1304	7.2941	7.4593	7.6260
27	6.2399	6.3968	6.5555	6.7160	6.8781	7.0419	7.2073	7.3743	7.5428
28	6.1512	6.3098	6.4702	6.6323	6.7961	6.9616	7.1287	7.2974	7.4676
29	6.0700	6.2302	6.3921	6.5558	6.7213	6.8884	7.0572	7.2276	7.3995
30	5.9955	6.1572	6.3207	6.4860	6.6530	6.8218	6.9921	7.1641	7.3376

Subject Property Net Income		$12,010
Comparables Indicate Cash Flow Rate		10.2%
Best Available Mortgage Financing for Subject:		
Loan Value Ratio		90%
Interest Rate	6.75%	
Initial Curtail	1.50%	
MIP	0.50%	
Debt Service Rate	8.75%	

The rate of cash flow to equity can be used to develop an overall capitalization rate, as follows:

Debt Service Rate of 8.75% x 90% Mortgage	7.875%
Cash Flow to Equity Rate of 10.2% x 10% Equity	1.020%
Overall Rate by Cash Flow Method	8.895%

Net Income of $12,010 divided by Rate of 8.895%=$135,000 Capitalized Value.

Cash Flow to Equity Example

A perfect example of the use of the Cash Flow to Equity formula to arrive at an estimated Market Value of a property in question, is the following analysis of Rudy's Market, located in Swansea, Massachusetts.

The Seller, Dan Durso, has given me permission to use the analysis of Rudy's Market in this book noted below:

October 14, 2002

To Whom It May Concern:

John V. Medeiros, of 89 Norwood Street, Swansea, Massachusetts, prepared an analysis for me of Rudy's Market, Wilbur Avenue, Swansea, Massachusetts.

The report, or analysis, estimated the market value of Rudy's Market, at the time of the report, based on hypothetical estimated future income and financing considerations.

John is asking for my permission to include the analysis in his forthcoming book "The Bucks Begin Here."

I do hereby grant permission for John V. Medeiros, of 89 Norwood Street, Swansea, Massachusetts to include the analysis of Rudy's Market in his forthcoming book "The Bucks Begin Here."

Daniel Durso

Dianne L Durso
Witness

The Estimated Market Value for this property was five hundred fifty thousand dollars ($550,000) according to the analysis.

The property sold for five hundred thousand dollars ($500,000), within two months, to the owner of Lil Audrey's Store, in Somerset, Massachusetts.

Both the Seller, Dan Durso, and the buyer of the property were very satisfied with the following analysis.

Please note that certain exhibits included in the analysis made for the seller are not included, namely the tax record, profit and loss statements, and inventory of equipment, as these were not deemed necessary for the illustrative purposes of this book.

Exhibits Used for Analysis of Rudy's Market, Swansea, Massachusetts:
  *tax record
  *plat map
  *flood plain map showing location of the subject property
  *resumé of John V. Medeiros
  table of conventional loan factors
  *profit and loss statements
  *inventory of equipment
  Exterior photos of Rudy's Market
  *Rudy's takeout menus
  additional tables and loan factors
Note: those items marked with an asterisk (*) are not included with this report, as they have no pertinent bearing on the analysis but are "back up" material included with the original analysis submitted.

TELEPHONE
673-3385
AREA CODE 508

89 NORWOOD STREET
SWANSEA, MASS.
ZIP 02777

JOHN V. MEDEIROS
CSR, CPA, BSA
ASSOCIATED INVESTMENTS

CERTIFIED REAL ESTATE APPRAISER
MASS. LICENSE NO. 244
RHODE ISLAND LICENSE NO. A00184R

REAL ESTATE APPRAISALS & SALES		INSURANCE-LIFE & HEALTH
LICENSED BROKER—MASS, RI.	CONSULTANT	LICENSED GENERAL AGENT
CERTIFIED SENIOR APPRAISER-AACA	NURSING HOMES	MASSACHU-SETTS & RI.
CERTIFIED REVIEW APPRAISER-NA BA/MU	MULTIFAMILY HOUSING	HUD/FHA FEE APPRAISER
RESIDENTIAL. COMMERCIAL, INDUSTRIAL EVALUATIONS	VA FEE APPRAISER	

To: All Interested Buyers
            Market Analysis

Subject: Estimated Market Value of Rudy's Country Market
            Properties Located at
            395 Wilbur Avenue
            Swansea, Massachusetts 02777

The purpose of this analysis is to determine the estimated value of the subject properties, based solely on the income approach to value. Note: this report is not a "commercial" appraisal.

Determination of estimated Market Value is made by three approaches to value, namely:

Cost Approach, which requires the use of depreciation estimates. The Cost approach has very little relevance in this valuation, due to the age, condition, amount of improvements, and the difficulty in estimating an accurate accrued depreciation estimate. Therefore, the Cost Approach is unreliable in this case and is omitted from this valuation.

The Sales Comparison Approach has not been utilized due to the many variables, this is a medium size meat and grocery market and true comparables are nonexistent.

Therefore, the only accurate method of determining value is solely by the Income Approach, where the net income of the property combined with the latest financing arrangements, will show the maximum mortgage obtainable, the equity investment required, with desired rate of equity return. This method will thus be used to obtain the market value of the subject property.

The Income Approach to value is usually the most applicable approach, and the determination of value based on the net income makes the most sense, after all, the income is what supports the mortgage, and is the more valid approach.

Therefore, I utilized the Income Approach solely, in my analysis.
Rudy's Country Market exhibits great income potential, as there is no other meat market in the vicinity, and no room, or land available to build in that area.

Properly run, this a potential "gold mine".

The estimated market value is based solely on the income approach, with financial and other data provided to me by my client, Daniel R. Durso, Trustee of Aspen Associates Realty Trust, 65 Aspen Drive, Bridgewater, Massachusetts.

In the Income-Capitalization Approach, which I utilized, certain considerations are considered, including:

Annual potential estimated income: that is what is obtainable in the marketplace and not necessarily the present income.

Annual expenses, capital rate derivation, obtainable financing with current terms.

Book depreciation is not considered: the present worth of the anticipated net annual income flow is determined by an overall capitalization rate determined by the cash flow to equity method as shown in the following pages.

Financing is assumed available at competitive mortgage interest rates.

A recent study of the present Market revealed that current financing is available as follows:

One bank quoted a 6 3/4% interest rate for 20 years and 20% down, while another bank quoted an 8% interest rate for 15 years and 30% down.

Financing for this type of property could probably be available for a 20 year financing at a 70% mortgage rate, with 30% equity (down payment) at between a 6 3/4% to 8% interest rate, depending on the Banking Institution.

After inquiries to knowledgeable parties in the field, I have arrived at the following, in order to arrive at a capitalized value of the property.

Assumed available:
Mortgage Term: 20 years at an interest rate of 8%
Mortgage Ratio: 70% of estimated Market Value of the Property.
Equity. (down payment): 30% of the Estimated Value of Property.

Capitalization Data:
Interest Rate: 8% see Table below:

Conventional Loan Payment Factors For Monthly Payments Per $1,000

Years	Rate 7	7.25	7.5	7.75	8	8.25	8.5	8.75	9
1	86.5267	86.6420	86.7574	86.8729	86.9884	87.1041	87.2198	87.3356	87.4515
2	44.7726	44.8860	44.9996	45.1134	45.2273	45.3414	45.4557	45.5701	45.6847
3	30.8771	30.9915	31.1062	31.2212	31.3364	31.4518	31.5675	31.6835	31.7997
4	23.9462	24.0624	24.1789	24.2957	24.4129	24.5304	24.6483	24.7665	24.8850
5	19.8012	19.9194	20.0379	20.1570	20.2764	20.3963	20.5165	20.6372	20.7584
6	17.0490	17.1693	17.2901	17.4114	17.5332	17.6556	17.7784	17.9017	18.0255
7	15.0927	15.2152	15.3383	15.4620	15.5862	15.7111	15.8365	15.9625	16.0891
8	13.6337	13.7585	13.8839	14.0099	14.1367	14.2641	14.3921	14.5208	14.6502
9	12.5063	12.6333	12.7610	12.8895	13.0187	13.1487	13.2794	13.4108	13.5429
10	11.6108	11.7401	11.8702	12.0011	12.1328	12.2653	12.3986	12.5327	12.6676
11	10.8841	11.0156	11.1480	11.2813	11.4154	11.5505	11.6864	11.8232	11.9608
12	10.2838	10.4176	10.5523	10.6879	10.8245	10.9621	11.1006	11.2400	11.3803
13	9.7807	9.9167	10.0537	10.1917	10.3307	10.4708	10.6118	10.7538	10.8968
14	9.3540	9.4922	9.6314	9.7718	9.9132	10.0557	10.1992	10.3438	10.4894
15	8.9883	9.1286	9.2701	9.4128	9.5565	9.7014	9.8474	9.9945	10.1427
16	8.6721	8.8146	8.9583	9.1032	9.2493	9.3965	9.5449	9.6945	9.8452
17	8.3966	8.5412	8.6871	8.8342	8.9826	9.1321	9.2829	9.4349	9.5880
18	8.1550	8.3017	8.4497	8.5990	8.7496	8.9015	9.0546	9.2089	9.3644
19	7.9419	8.0907	8.2408	8.3922	8.5450	8.6991	8.8545	9.0111	9.1690
20	7.7530	7.9038	8.0559	8.2095	**8.3644**	8.5207	8.6782	8.8371	8.9973
21	7.5847	7.7375	7.8917	8.0473	8.2043	8.3627	8.5224	8.6834	8.8458
22	7.4342	7.5889	7.7451	7.9027	8.0618	8.2222	8.3841	8.5472	8.7117
23	7.2992	7.4558	7.6139	7.7735	7.9345	8.0970	8.2609	8.4261	8.5927
24	7.1776	7.3361	7.4960	7.6576	7.8205	7.9850	8.1508	8.3181	8.4866
25	7.0678	7.2281	7.3899	7.5533	7.7182	7.8845	8.0523	8.2214	8.3920
26	6.9684	7.1304	7.2941	7.4593	7.6260	7.7942	7.9638	8.1348	8.3072
27	6.8781	7.0419	7.2073	7.3743	7.5428	7.7128	7.8842	8.0570	8.2313
28	6.7961	6.9616	7.1287	7.2974	7.4676	7.6393	7.8125	7.9871	8.1630
29	6.7213	6.8884	7.0572	7.2276	7.3995	7.5729	7.7477	7.9240	8.1016
30	6.6530	6.8218	6.9921	7.1641	7.3376	7.5127	7.6891	7.8670	8.0462

20 years at 8% interest results in a factor of 8,3644 (monthly). Multiply 8.3644 x 12 for one year=8.3644 x 12=100.3728, which, divided by 1000=0.1003728 (10.03728) Debt service Rate.

Under the Cash Flow to Equity, the Rate can be utilized to develop an overall capitalization rate as follows:

Debt Service Rate: 0.1003728 x 0.70 (705 Mortgage)=7.026%

Cash flow to equity rate: 30% multiplied by expected Equity Return of 8%=30 x 0.08=2.4% Thus: 7.026+2.4=9.426, which yields a 0.094260 overall capitalization rate by the Cash Flow to Equity Method.

Based on Net Income derived from Estimated Potential Profit and Loss, the Capitalized Value of the Subject Property, (assuming 8% Interest Rate, 20 year Term, 70% Mortgage, 305 Equity) is as follows:

Net Income Estimated of $50,000, divided by Overall Capitalization Rate of 0.09426=$530,448 Estimated value of the Property

PROOF: $530,448 x 70% Mortgage   =$530,448 x 0.70= $371,314
               $530,448 x 30% Equity   =$530,448 x 0.30= $159,134
                                       Total $530,448
                                                 (checks with above).

The previous example utilized an 8% Interest Rate with a 20 year Term and a 70% Mortgage. This would be at the high end of Interest.

The next example will show what the Value would be with a 6 3/4% Interest Rate, 20 year Term, 70 % Mortgage, 30 %Equity, with an 8% Equity Return:

Utilizing the Mortgage Tables for 6 3/4% interest for 20 years:

7.60 x 12 (months)=91.2, divided by 1000=9.12% Debt Service Rate

9.12 x 0.70 (70% mortgage)   =   6.384%
8.0 Equity x 30% Equity (0.30)   =   <u>2.4 %</u>
                   Return: 8.784% Overall Capitalization Rate

Estimated Potential Net Income: $50,000 divided by 0.08784=$569,216

<u>SUMMARY</u>

We now have a range of Estimated Values based on different obtainable Interest Rates:

At 6 3/4% Interest Rate the Estimated Value   = $569,216

At 8% Interest Rate the Estimated Value   = $530, 448

This analysis indicates that the market value of the subject property is:
Five hundred and fifty thousand dollars ($550,000) <u>as is</u>.

Real estate broker: John V. Medeiros
Massachusetts Licensed and Rhode Island Licensed

<u>Note</u>: this report is not a "commercial" appraisal. It is an analysis of anticipated net income, resulting in an estimate of the maximum mortgage which is obtainable at various interest rates and terms.

How To Sell One Of Your Homes Every Two Years Without Capital Gains

Under public law 105-34, the taxpayer relief act, signed by President Clinton on August 5, 1997, you can sell your primary home and exclude as much as $250,000 of your profit if you are single, or $500,000 if you are married, filing a joint federal income tax return. But to qualify for the full exclusion, you must have owned the home and lived in it as your primary residence for two of the five years prior to the sale. Thus, you theoretically could sell your home this year, claim the full exclusion, move into another home, live in it for two years as your primary residence and repeat the process two years later. There is no limit to the number of times you may use this exclusion.

Treasury officials say that this law effectively means most Americans can sell their primary residence without worrying about paying capital gains taxes on the profits. However, if you lose money on the sale of your home, you can't deduct the losses.

Two to Four Family Evaluation

The income or rent obtainable from two to four family residences has a very important bearing in estimating their value. The income derived from the rental of family apartments varies, even with the same amenities. This is due to location. A good property location is reflected by the rents charged; a better location will command more rent than a poorer location.

In evaluating a prospective property, the rents presently charged to the occupying tenants are not necessarily the market rents that are obtainable. This may be due to the rental to family members or friends, which generally bring a lower rent than that obtainable in the marketplace.

To find out what the proper, obtainable rent should be, you should visit the public library, a friendly real estate broker, or an assessor's office and ask for permission to look through the multiple listing of sold properties book. The multiple listing book has properties recently sold, categorized by city or town under the headings of two family, three family, and four or more family. Some, but not all properties sold, show the rents that are being charged, listing the total number of rooms, bedrooms, and baths for the apartments, along with other pertinent data. The rents shown are those charged, without utilities, as it is assumed that the tenant pays for electricity, heat and telephone. The landlord or owner generally pays for water and sewer charges. The sales price and the date sold are also listed.

When the sales price is divided by the total monthly rent received, the factor derived is called the Gross Rent Multiplier.

For example:

A three family property sold for $150,000 at a recent date (within 6 months). The rents charged per month (no utilities) for three units were $475, $500, and $525 for a total, of $1500 for the 3 units. Dividing the sale price of $150,000 by the total monthly rent of $1500 results in a factor of 100. This is called the Gross Rent Multiplier.

Now, scanning the sold book, in the 3 family category and utilizing the data from similar 3 family properties that show the same number of bedrooms, try to use those comparable sales that are located near the subject property, if possible, as location has an important bearing on obtainable rents. Make a list of the gross rent multipliers obtained from these comparable sales. From this list utilize the Gross Rent Multipliers that appear more often, giving more weight to an average of these. For example, if the Gross Rent Multipliers obtained from six properties are: 115, 110, 100, 100, 98, and 95, then the gross rent multiplier of 100 is the most appropriate.

If the market rents obtainable from a 3 family residence are $1500 per month (no utilities provided), then $1500 x 100 Gross Rent Multiplier results in $150,000. This is a good way to estimate what the property is worth!

Another way to estimate the value of 2 to 4 family residences is by using comparable sales. Again, looking through the Comparable Sales book, under the type sold (one family, two family, three family, or four or more family), compare the properties sold with the property in question. In looking through the comparable sales, try to get as many similar characteristics as the subject: same number of bedrooms, total rooms, sale within past 6 months, and proximity to the subject. This will give you a range of values for the 3 family-property that you are evaluating. Do the same with the 2 family and 4 or more unit sales for those types of properties you would like to evaluate. Do not try to compare the evaluation of a 3 unit (3 family) property with a sold 2 family property. This would be not comparing, 'apples with apples'.

By means of the comparable sales and the Gross Rent Multipliers income evaluation you should have a good idea what the prospective property is worth. However, it is worth repeating, if you believe that the property you are looking at is worth buying, then you should obtain a professional appraisal by a licensed appraiser. The bank will require an official appraisal in order for you to obtain financing. This will also give you protection against unknowns, which will be brought out in the appraisal.

If you don't feel comfortable in doing your own thing, a good method would be to contact an active, knowledgeable real estate broker to show you a list of properties that are for sale. A good real estate broker will give you your money 's worth. The broker will provide you with a market analysis of the type of property that you are looking for and physically show you what is out there for sale. A good broker will also help you find the right financing and save you many steps and perhaps missteps. A listing contract will be drawn up with all the particulars of the agreement. Usually, a three-month contract is sufficient. If you find that you are not satisfied with the broker's service, don't extend the contract!

When performing an appraisal a licenses appraiser has to look at many things such as:

- Is the zoning legal?
- Is the lot area sufficient, if building a new home?
- Is the property in a flood plain?
- Are there any environmental problems inherent in the property or in the property area?
- What utilities are available?
- Do the water supply and the septic or sewer system provide adequate service?
- What is the availability of schools, transportation, and other amenities?
- What are the market conditions?
- What is the comparison of sales of the type desired with the necessary adjustments to arrive at an estimated market value?

The universal residential report that must be filled out, called the URAR form, has many items that must be addressed.

Along with a professional appraisal, an inspection by a licensed home inspector is important, to show what the condition of the subject property is at that time. Termite and perhaps a radon inspection may also be required.

How To Save Thousands Of Dollars In Savings On Your Mortgage Interest

1. Make biweekly payments

2. If you can afford the extra monthly payments, take out a 15-year mortgage instead of a typical 30-year mortgage

3. Make regular monthly payments, but realize huge savings by making biweekly payments

You pay half of your regular monthly payment every two weeks. For example, instead of paying your scheduled payment of $1,000 per month, you pay $500 every two weeks. Thus, instead of paying $12,000 for the year (12 months at $1,000 per month), you pay $13,000 for the year (26 weeks at $500 per week). This results in an additional $1,000 payment per year.

Under a biweekly schedule, a $100,000 mortgage at 10.5 % is paid off in 20.5 years, instead of 30 years, with an interest saving of $85,843!

Some banks refuse to allow biweekly payments. In that case, look around, there are plenty of banks to choose from.

The following examples will show you the savings obtainable by utilizing biweekly payment mortgages.

Example 1. $100,000 loan, 30 year term at 8 % interest

	Monthly Payments	Biweekly Payments
Amount of payment	$734	$367
Number of yearly payments	12	26
Total annual payment	$8,805	$9,539
Total interest	$164,149	$117,848
Interest saved	$ 0	$46,301

Thus, on a 30-year term loan of $100,000 at 8% interest, the savings obtained by the use of a biweekly payment schedule would be $46,301.

Example 2. $100,000 loan, 30 year term at 9% interest

	Monthly Payments	Biweekly Payments
Amount of payment	$805	$402
Number of yearly payments	12	26
Total annual payment	$9,656	$10,460

	Monthly Payments	Biweekly Payments
Actual term years	30	21.923
Total interest	$189,654	$129,237
Interest saved	$ 0	$60,417

Thus, on a 30-year term loan of $100,000 at 9% interest, the savings obtained by the use of a biweekly payment schedule would be $60,417.

Example 3. $ 100,000 loan, 30 year term at 10% interest

	Monthly Payments	Biweekly Payments
Amount of payment	$878	$439
Number yearly payments	12	26
Total annual payment	$10,531	$11,409
Actual term years	30	20.962
Total interest	$215,909	$139,104
Interest saved	$ 0	$76,806

Thus, on a 30-year term loan of $100,000 at 10% interest, the savings obtained by the use of a biweekly payment schedule would be $76,806.

Example 4. $1000,000 loan, 30 year term at 10.5% interest

	Monthly Payments	Biweekly Payments
Amount of payment	$915	$457
Number of yearly payments	12	26
Total annual payment	$10,997	$11,892

Total interest	$229,304	$143,461
Interest saved	$ 0	$85,843

Thus, on a 30-year term loan of $100,000 at 10.5% interest, the savings obtained by the use of a biweekly payment schedule would be $85,843.

How do you like those apples!

Homeowners can save thousands of dollars by means of biweekly mortgage payments. They held the borrower and the lender by paying off the principal faster.

This is mortgage payment method that is quicker and cheaper than conventional loans. Everything can be done automatically. You don't even have to write checks.

There is no trick or magic involved. For example, instead of making monthly payments of $500, the borrower pays $250 every two weeks. Because there are 52 weeks in a year, biweekly payments result in 26 annual payments. Thus, the homeowner makes the equivalent of 13 monthly payments in-a year.

Payments can be made with ease. Every two weeks the lending institution automatically withdraws the money from the borrower's account, eliminating the chore of writing checks and checking statements. All the borrower has to do is have extra money in the account to ensure that there is enough money to be withdrawn. Although it may not seem like much at first, the biweekly payments build up equity at a faster rate than normal monthly mortgage payments. The principal is reduced faster and interest expenses are sharply curtailed. For example, biweekly payments would save a homeowner $78,377 on a $100,00 mortgage at a fixed rate of 10%, and the loan would be paid off in 21 years instead of 30 years.

It gets even better! The greater the principal and the higher the interest rate, the more money saved.

At 12% interest, a–biweekly mortgage payment would pay off, a $100,000, 30 year mortgage in 19 years. At 13% percent interest, even a $50,000 mortgage would be $79,935 less costly in interest payments.

As interest rates crawl upward, the appeal of the biweekly payment has increased. Thousands of inquiries have flooded the Washington offices of the Federal National Mortgage Association, known as Fannie Mae, since it decided in January 1988 to support the biweekly payment.

Fannie Mae is a federal corporation that purchases mortgages from banks and sells them on a secondary market as securities. Fannie Mae estimated, at that time, that a quarter of a billion dollars, most of it in the northeast, had been lent out as biweeklies.

The biweekly should catch on, because it is a win for everyone. From the lender's perspective, it is a win because the history of biweekly is that it has fewer delinquencies. From the borrower's standpoint, it is a painless way of paying off the mortgage faster.

Several advantages accrue from offering biweekly mortgages: more frequent payments which improve a bank's cash flow, while the faster repayment schedule means the lending institution will have the money earlier to loan again.

Contact your friendly banker. The huge savings are worth the effort.

Homeowner's Insurance

Ways To Lower Your Homeowners Insurance Costs

Insurance is a highly competitive business and the price you pay for your homeowner's insurance can vary by hundreds of dollars, depending on the insurance company you buy your policy from. Companies offer several types of discounts, but they don't offer the same discount or the same amount of discount in all states. That is why you should ask your agent or company's representative about any discounts available. Here are some things to consider when buying homeowners insurance:

1. <u>Be sure to shop around</u>. It will take a few phone calls, but they could save you a good sum of money. Ask your friends, check the yellow pages, check consumer guides, call insurance agents and companies or call your state insurance department. Call the National Insurance Consumer Helpline (HICH) at 1-800-942-4242 for more information. They can also tell you how to reach your state insurance department.. This will give you an idea of price ranges and tell you which companies or agents have the lowest prices. However, do not consider price alone. The insurer you select should offer a fair price and excellent service. Quality service may cost a bit more, but it provides added conveniences, so talk to a number of insurers to get a feeling for the type of service they provide. Ask them what they would do to lower your costs. Check the financial ratings of the companies, too. Then, when you-have narrowed the field to three insurers, get price quotes.

2. <u>Raise your deductible</u>. Deductibles are the amount of money you have to pay toward a loss before your insurance company starts to pay, according to the terms of your policy. Deductibles on homeowners' policies typically start at $250. Increasing your deductible to $500, could save you up to 12 percent; $1,000, up to 24 percent; $2,500, up to 30 percent, and $5,000, up to 37 percent, depending upon your insurance company.

3. <u>Buy your home and automobile policies from the same insurer</u>. Some companies that sell homeowners and automobile, and liability coverage will take 5 to 15 percent off of your premium if you buy two or more policies from them.

4. <u>When you buy a home consider how much insuring it will cost</u>. Because a new home's electrical heating and plumbing and overall structure are likely to be in better shape than those of an older house, insurers may offer you a discount of 8 to 15 percent if your house is new. Check its construction, too. Brick, because of its resistance to wind damage, is better in the East. Frame construction, because of its resistance to earthquake damage, is better in the West. Choosing wisely could cut your premiums by 5 to 15 percent. Avoiding areas that are prone to floods can save you $400 or so a year in flood insurance. Homeowners' insurance does not cover flood-related damage. If you do buy a house in a flood prone area, you will also have to buy a flood insurance policy. Does your house have full time or volunteer fire service? Is your house close to a fire hydrant or fire station? The closer your house is to firefighters and their equipment, the lower your premium will be.

5. <u>Insure your house, not the land</u>. The land under your house isn't at risk from theft, windstorm, fire, and other perils covered in your homeowners' policy, so don't include its value in deciding how much homeowners insurance to buy. If you do, you will pay a much higher premium than you should. Typically, the land value of a home property is approximately 30 to 40 percent of the total home value. For example, a home valued at $120,000, will have usually have a land value of between 30%($36,000) to 40 % ($48,000). The insurance company will not cover you for any amount over the building value.

6. <u>Check you home security</u>. You can usually get discounts of at least 5 percent for a smoke detector, burglar alarm, or dead bolt locks. Some companies offer to cut your premium by as much as 15 to 20 percent if you install a sophisticated fire sprinkler system and a fire and burglar alarm that rings at the police station or other monitoring facility. These systems are not cheap and not every system qualifies for the discount. Before you buy such a system, find out what kind your insurer

recommends and how much the device would cost and how much you would save on the premiums.

7. <u>Don't smoke</u>. Smoking accounts for more than 23,000 residential fires a year. That is why some insurers offer to reduce premiums if all the residents in a house don't smoke.

8. <u>Seek out discounts for seniors</u>. Retired people stay at home and detect trouble sooner than working people. Retired people also have more time for maintaining their homes. If you are at least 55 years old and retired, you may qualify for a discount of up to 10 percent from some insurance companies.

9. <u>See if you can get group coverage</u>. Employers, alumni, and business associates often work out an insurance package with an insurance company at very competitive rates. Ask your company's personal manager or your association's director if such a package is available to you.

10. <u>Stay with the same insurer</u>. If you have kept your coverage with a company for several years, you may receive special consideration. Several insurers will reduce their premiums by 5 percent if you stay with them for three to five years and by 10 percent if you remain a policyholder for six years or more.

11. <u>Compare the limits in your policy and the value of your possessions at least once a year</u>. You may want your policy to cover any major purchases or additions to your home, but you do not want to spend money for coverage you don't need. If your five-year-old fur coat is no longer worth the $20,000 you paid for it, you will want to reduce your floater and pocket the difference.

12. <u>Look for private insurance first</u>. If you live in a high-risk area (one that is especially vulnerable to coastal storms, fires, or crime) and you have been buying your homeowners insurance through a government plan, you should check with an insurance agent or company representative. You may find that there are steps you can take that will allow you to buy

insurance at a lower price in the private market. If you have questions about insurance for any of your possessions, be sure to ask your agent or company representative when you are shopping around for a policy. For example, if you are like the steadily increasing number of people who are running a business out of their home, be sure to discuss coverage for that business. Most homeowners' policies cover only up to $2500 of business equipment in the home, and they offer no business liability insurance. Although you want to lower your homeowners' insurance cost, you also want to make certain you have all the coverage you need.

Shop Around For The Best Mortgage

Shopping, comparing, and negotiating may save you many thousands of dollars. Shopping around for a home loan or mortgage will help you to get the best financing deal. A mortgage, whether it is a home purchase, a refinancing, or a home equity loan, is a product, just like a car, so the price and terms may be negotiable. You will want to compare all the costs involved in obtaining a mortgage.

Obtain Information From Several Lenders

Different lenders may quote you different prices, so you should contact several lenders to make sure you are getting the best price. Home loans are available from several types of lenders: commercial banks, thrift institutions, mortgage companies and credit unions.

You can also get a home loan through a mortgage broker. Brokers arrange transactions rather than lending money directly. They will find a lender for you. A broker's access to several lenders can mean a wider selection of loan products and terms from which you can choose. Brokers will generally contact several lenders, regarding your application but they are not obligated to find the best deal for you unless they have contracted with you to act as your agent. Thus, you should consider contacting more than one broker, just as you should investigate more than one bank or thrift institution.

Whether you are dealing with a lender or a broker may not always be clear. Some financial institutions operate as both lenders and brokers: and most broker advertisements do not use the word "broker ". Therefore be sure to ask whether a broker is involved. This information is important because brokers are usually paid a fee for their services that may be separate from and in addition to the lender's origination or other fees. A broker's compensation may be in the form of 'points' paid at closing or as an addition on your interest-rate-or-both. You should ask each broker you work with how he or she will be compensated so that you can compare the different fees. Be prepared to negotiate with the brokers as well as the lenders.

Obtain All Important Cost Information

Be sure to get information about mortgages from several lenders or brokers. Know how much of a down payment you can afford, and find out all the costs involved in the loan. Knowing just the amount of the monthly payment or the interest rate is-not-enough. Ask for information about the same loan amount, loan term, and type of loan, so that you can compare the information.

The following information is important to get from each lender and broker:

Rates

Ask each lender or broker for a list of its current mortgage interest rates and whether the rates being quoted are the lowest for that day or week.

Ask whether the rate is fixed or adjustable. Keep in mind that when interest rates for adjustable rate loans go up, generally so does the monthly payment.

If the rate quoted is for an adjustable-rate loan, ask how your rate and loan payment will vary: including whether your loan payment will be reduced when rates go down.

Ask about the loan's annual percentage rate (APR). The APR takes into account not only the interest rate, but also points, broker fees, and certain other credit charges that you may be required to pay. This is expressed as a yearly rate.

Points

Points are fees paid to the lender or broker and are often linked to the interest rate. Usually, the more points you pay the lower the rate.

Check your local newspaper for information about rates and points currently being offered.

Ask for points to be quoted to you as a dollar amount rather than just as the number of points so that you will actually know how much you will have to pay.

Fees

A home loan often involves many fees, such as loan origination or underwriting fees, broker fees, and transaction, settlement, and closing costs.

Every lender or broker should be able to give you an estimate of its fees. Many of these fees are negotiable.

Some fees are paid when you apply for a loan (such as application and appraisal fees), and others are paid at closing. In some cases, you can borrow the money needed to pay these fees, but doing so will increase your loan amount and total costs.

"No cost" loans are sometimes available but they usually involve higher rates.

Ask what each fee includes, as several items may be lumped into one fee.

Ask for an explanation of any fee you do not understand.

Down Payments-And-Private-Mortgage-Insurance

Some lenders require 20 percent of the home's purchase price as a down payment. However, many lenders now offer loans that require less than 20 percent down, sometimes as little as 5 percent on conventional-loans. If a 20 percent down payment is not made, lenders usually require the homebuyer to purchase private-mortgage-insurance (PMI), to protect the lender in case the homebuyer fails to pay.

When government assisted programs such as FHA (federal housing administration), or rural development services are available, the down payment requirements may be substantially smaller.

Ask about the lender's requirements for a down payment, including what you need to do to verify that funds for your down payment are available.

Ask your lender about special programs it may offer. If PMI is required for your loan ask what the total cost of the insurance will be. Ask-how much your monthly payment will be when including the PMI premium, and ask how long you will be required to carry PMI.

Negotiate For The Best Deal That You Can

Once you know what each lender has to offer, negotiate for the best deal. On any given day, lenders and brokers may offer different prices for the same loan terms to different consumers, even if those consumers have the same qualifications. The most likely reason for this difference in price is that loan officers and brokers are often allowed to keep some or all of this difference as extra compensation.

Generally, the difference between the lowest available price for a loan product and any higher price that the borrower agrees to pay is called an <u>overage</u>. When overages occur, they are built into the prices quoted to consumers. They can occur in both fixed and variable-rate loans and can be in the form of points, fees, or the interest rate. Whether quoted to you by a loan officer or broker, the price of any loan may contain overages.

Have the lender or broker write down all the costs associated with the loan, then ask if the lender or broker will waive or reduce one or more of its fees or agree to a lower rate or fewer points. You will want to make sure that the lender or broker is not agreeing to lower one fee while raising another or to lower the rate while raising points. There is no harm in asking lenders or brokers if they can give better terms than the original ones they quoted or than those you have found elsewhere.

Once you are satisfied with the terms you have negotiated, you may want to obtain a written <u>lock-in</u> from the lender or broker. The lock-in should include the rate that you have agreed to pay, the period the lock-in lasts, and the number of points to be paid. A fee may be charged for locking in the loan rate. This fee may be refundable at closing. Lock-ins can protect you from rate increases while your loan is being processed: if rates fall, however, you could end up with a less favorable rate. Should that happen, try to reach a compromise with the lender or broker.

Remember: Shop, Compare, Negotiate

When buying a home, remember to shop around, to compare costs and terms, and to negotiate for the best deal.

Your local newspaper and the Internet are good places to start shopping for a loan. You can usually find information both on interest rates and on points for several lenders. Since rates and points can change daily, you will want to check your newspaper often when shopping for a home loan. But the newspaper does not list the fees, so be sure to ask the lenders about them.

Don't be afraid to make lenders and brokers compete with each other for your business by letting them know that you are shopping for the best deal.

Fair Lending

Fair lending-is-required-by-law.

The equal credit opportunity act prohibits lenders from discriminating against credit applicants in any aspect of a credit transaction on the basis of race, color, religion, national origin, sex, marital status, age, whether all or part of the applicant's income comes from a public assistance program, or whether the applicant has in good faith exercised a right under the consumer protection act.

The fair housing act-prohibits discrimination in residential real estate transactions, on the basis of race, color, religion, sex, disability, familial status, or national origin.

Under these laws, a consumer cannot be refused a loan based on these characteristics nor be charged more for a loan or offered less favorable terms on such characteristics.

Credit Problems?

If you have credit problems you should still shop, compare and negotiate. Do not assume that minor credit problems or difficulties stemming from unique circumstances, such as illness, or temporary loss of income, will limit your loan choices to only high-cost lenders.

If your credit report contains negative information that is accurate, but there are good reasons for trusting you to repay a loan, be sure to explain your situation to the lender or broker. If your credit problems cannot be explained, you will probably have to pay more than borrowers who have good credit histories. However, do not assume that the only way to get credit is to pay a high price. Ask how your past credit history affects the price of your loan and what you

would need to do to get a better price. Take the time to shop around and negotiate the best deal that you can.

Whether you have credit problems or not, it is a good idea to review your
credit report for accuracy and completeness before you apply for a loan.

To order a copy of your credit report, you can contact one of the following:

Equifax: (800) 685-1111

Trans-Union: (800) 916-8800

Experian: (800) 682-7654

Real Estate Taxes

Are You Over-Paying Your Taxes?

Are You Being Over-Assessed?

You may be paying more in real estate taxes than you should. How to find out? Do it yourself!

Check your tax bill and compare it with the taxes paid by your neighbors and those within a mile of your home. Check only those properties that have a similar design as your home. For example, if your house is a ranch, only obtain data on similar ranch style homes. See the diagram at the end of this section on "How to Measure Your House" which illustrates various designs.

What you are going to do is called a market analysis, which is less complex than an appraisal. It will give you enough information to let you decide if you believe you are being over-assessed and therefore, over-taxed.

One of the items that you will be looking for is the gross living area of the comparable properties as compared to the gross living area of your home.

Gross living area is obtained by measuring the outside area of your building, as demonstrated in the illustration at the end of this section. Measure (in feet) the outside of the main building, multiplying the length by the width. Add to that the square footage of any additions such as the "Wing" in the illustration. Length x Width=Sq. Ft. (Square Feet).

If the building has two full floors, add the square footage of the second floor to that of the first floor, then add any additional areas to obtain the Total Gross Living Area.

In order to be classified as Gross Living Area, the measured areas must be heated and "above ground", Being "above ground" means that where the foundation meets the outside land, the floor must be at or above that level. For example: A "Raised Ranch" could have its lower level completely finished, but if any part of that lower level is below the outside level, it is not considered Gross Living Area.

The finished gross living area will have an Amenity value, such as $3,000 to a low of about $500, depending on the percentage of finished area. Extra "frills" incorporated into the home are of value to the present owner only. Possible buyers would probably not be willing to pay extra for the "frills".

Raised Ranches and Bi-level homes have Gross Living Area only on the second level for the Raised Ranch and on the second and third levels for the Bi-level. The first level in a Raised Ranch is called the basement, because it is below ground.

A "Cape" has one and one half levels. Add one half of the Gross Living Area of the first level (above the basement) to the Gross Living Area of the first level to obtain the total Gross Living Area. A "Colonial" has twice the first level area.

An easy way to obtain the Gross Living Area of your home, and that of the "comparables" you are going to use, is to visit your assessor's office and ask for a copy of the Field Cards (also called Property Cards), for your home and that of the "comparable " homes you will be using for comparison to your home.

The Field Cards will have all the data that you need in order to compare your home to that of the comparables, such as name and address, plot and lot and deed book and page reference, gross living area, number of rooms, bedrooms, baths, with a description of the interior and exterior materials, type of heat, garages, if any, etc. The Field Card will also have the "Assessed Value" of the land and building separately and the Total Assessed Value, with the corresponding tax levied.

The Assessed Value is not necessarily the "Fair Market Value" of the property. Due to sales price changes over the years, the previously assigned values at the time of town revaluation when estimated values are brought up to date, there will be a difference between the assessed value and that of the Fair Market Value of the home in question sometimes reaching a ratio of over 50%, where the home is assessed at less than half the possible sale obtainable price. So, the Assessed Value may have no true indication of what that home could sell for in today's market. However, by comparing your assessed value to that of the "comparables" you can then determine whether or not you are being over-assessed, and thus over-paying your real estate tax.

Example: A home assessed at a total of $75,000 for both Land and Building, which has a probable Sale Value of $150,000, is assessed at 50% of fair market value.

However, what you are trying to do is to determine where the assessed values of the "comparables" and your home differ.

The Assessor's Office has a Location (Address) book that has the names, addresses, assessed value and taxes of every parcel in that city or town. If you find that your assessed value is larger than that of your "comparable" ask the Assessor or clerk for a copy of that particular Property Card.

Compare the Gross Living Area of the comparables to that of your home. See if they have approximately the same living area, within 500 square feet, then see what the assessed values are of the comparables and any differences between. Also check the amenities, such as a fireplace or garage, of the comparables against those of your home make adjustments to compare.

Usual adjustments are:

Gross Living Area	$20 per sq. ft. for homes under 25 years old.
	$15 per sq. ft. for homes over 25 to 50 years.
	$10 per sq. ft. for homes over 50 years old.
Fireplace	$1500 for an old fireplace to $3000 for a new one.
Garages	(under) range from $5000 for single space, under, to $10,000 single stall, attached (away from the building). These may vary, depending on the condition of the item in question.

Make the adjustments as follows; see "Grid" at the end of this article:

If the Comparable is better than the Subject (your home) then assign a minus adjustment. For example, if the Comparable is in a better location, a minus adjustment is made; If a Comparable's location is inferior to the Subject (your home) then a plus adjustment is made. Gross Living Area Adjustment: The subject (your home) has 1200 sq, ft. whereas a Comparable has 1100 Sq. ft., a difference of 100 sq. ft. Because the Subject's Living Area is more than the Comparable a plus adjustment of $2000 ($20 per sq. ft. x 100 sq. ft) is made. So, if your subject item is better than the Comparable make a plus adjustment is made; if the Comparable item is better, make a minus adjustment. After you have made all the adjustments, place in the Net Adjustment. (total) box, the differences between all of the plus adjustments and that of all the minus adjustments. Below that add the plus adjustments or subtract the minus adjustments from the Assessed value of the Comparable.

Average the resultant Comparables to that of the Subject (your home). If there is a large discrepancy, show this to your Assessor. Be sure to take photos (front and back) of your property and that of each Comparable.

Ask the assessor for an abatement. If your request is denied, and if you feel that you are being over-assessed, have an appraisal made (cost of $200 to $300). Then take this appraisal to the assessor. If your request for an abatement is still refused, then request an application to appear before the Appellate Tax Board of your State's Department of Taxation. They must provide you with an application. If the Assessor still refuses to grant you an abatement, then he, or his Board will have to appear at the Appellate Tax Board You will have to be present, or one designated by you, to present your case. You do not need a lawyer. Bring all the data that you have assembled, including the photos of the subject and the Comparables. When the taxpayer has done his "homework" the Appellate Tax Board will override the assessor and issue what a fair tax would be.

Here are a couple of examples to illustrate the aforementioned points:

Case 1:
As a State Certified Appraiser, I performed an Appraisal a few years ago in a nearby town. The owners were both deceased and the property was left to the sons. The granddaughter expressed an interest in the property. The property consisted of a Ranch, single family dwelling, along with an old garage and 25 Acres of Land. The property was assessed at $224,000. The heirs agreed to sell the property to the granddaughter for $149,000, believing that they were doing her a great favor. I appraised the property at $124,000 due to the fact that the property is in a flood plain, there are high voltage transmission lines diagonally

crossing the property and the subject had only a 100 foot frontage. The land was originally farmland, but there were now large trees and bushes where farmland used to be. Apparently, the assessor had valued the property many years ago when the farm was productive, which was no longer the case. I had good comparables for the building and assigned an amenity value of $500 an acre for their right to walk this excess land to the 24 acres remaining. After my explanation, the heirs approved. This may be a rare case, but the value was never updated.

Case 2:

An actual case to be heard by the Appellate Tax Board in Boston, Massachusetts is the following described appeal by Ferdinand and Claudia for real estate tax abatement. Little did I realize when I began writing this book that I would be involved in an actual case where the parties involved felt that they were over-assessed. They felt that the value placed on their property was not based on equal and uniform taxation. This case will involve me representing my daughter Claudia and her husband Ferdinand, before the appellate tax board, after being denied an abatement by the Swansea Board of Assessors. No lawyer is necessary as you can appeal your own case.

The letter addressed to the appellate tax board states the reasons for the appeal and lists comparable properties that are located on the next street over, those with similar lot sizes being given the most weight.

All the taxpayers are asking for is a fair evaluation. They are willing to pay a 15% increase to their former tax assessment, but not the 30% increase imposed by the town. I feel that they have a good case, there is an abundance of material that should show that the property was over assessed.

The appellate tax board has agreed to hear the case, it is identified as docket number 293943.

TELEPHONE   89 NORWOOD STREET
673-3385   SWANSEA, MASS.
AREA CODE 508   ZIP 02777

JOHN V. MEDEIROS
CSR, CPA, BSA
ASSOCIATED INVESTMENTS

CERTIFIED REAL ESTATE APPRAISER

MASS. LICENSE NO. 244

RHODE ISLAND LICENSE NO. A00184R

REAL ESTATE APPRAISALS & SALES	INSURANCE-LIFE & HEALTH	
LICENSED BROKER—MASS, RI.	CONSULTANT	LICENSED GENERAL AGENT
CERTIFIED SENIOR APPRAISER-AACA	NURSING HOMES	MASSACHU-SETTS & RI.
CERTIFIED REVIEW APPRAISER-NA BA/MU	MULTIFAMILY HOUSING	HUD/FHA FEE APPRAISER
RESIDENTIAL. COMMERCIAL, INDUSTRIAL EVALUATIONS	VA FEE APPRAISER	

To: Commonwealth of Massachusetts
           State Appellate Tax Board   Docket Number 293943
           Boston, Massachusetts

Subject: Appeal of denial of the Town of Swansea, Massachusetts
           For request for tax abatement by Ferdinand and Claudia
           Property located at 217 Main Drive
           Swansea, Massachusetts 02777

Gentlemen/Ladies:

Dear Board Members:

My name is John V. Medeiros, and I am the father of Claudia

And I am representing Ferdinand and Claudia in their appeal of the denial by
the Town of Swansea for a decrease in the present assessment, which they con-

sider unfair and incorrect. It is my opinion that the criteria of equal and uniform assessment have not been followed.

As a point of information, I served as an appraiser with the Massachusetts Bureau of Local Assessment, under Chief Edmund Giblin in 1967-1971. As you know, the purpose of the Bureau of Local Assessment is to ensure equal and uniform assessment of properties in the state of Massachusetts. I do have experience along those lines.

Meanwhile, I question the expertise of the reasoning of the Swansea Board of Assessors; the attached newspaper articles point out the inconsistencies and errors of the board. However, the reasons for this request for abatement are as follows:

1. The total assessed value was increased from $146,900 to $191,700, an increase of 30.4%

2. The assessed land value was increased from $54,000 to $84,900, an increase of 57.2%

3. Ratio of land value to total assessment is over 44% ($84,900/$191,700=0.4429)

   The ratio of 44+% of land to total assessment is excessive.

   GNMA and FNMA will not accept appraisals that exceed 35%, unless there is justification (waterfront property).

4. The average lot sale price of new developments in Windsor Court and Brentwood Court, which are located one street over from Main Drive, is $65,000. I would consider these new properties to be in a better location and in a higher price range than the properties on Main Drive. Yet, the ratio of land values average less than 30% of that of Main Drive: Most lots, subjects, and comparables are 30,000 square feet.

Subject: 217 Main Drive: land assessed at $84,900

properties at Windsor Court and Brentwood Court   land assessed at $65,000

Ratio of 130.6%   84,900/65,000=130.6 % (30+%)

5. Real estate values in Swansea increased by less than 15% as shown by:

   Town residential value year 2002= 890,834,115 tax rate l2.17 then 12.48
   Town residential value year 2001= 783,273,608 tax rate 13.39
   Increase in valuation   107,560,507

   Thus, the increase in town residential values was 890,834,155/783.272.608=1.1373, indicating an increase of 13.73%

6. Based on the above, the taxpayers, Ferdinand and Claudia are willing to pay their share by an increase of 15 % to the previous assessed value of $146,900 to $168,935

   Requested new assessment of $168,935 would be acceptable, as this would increase their tax by $275 ($274.99)and reduce the present tax by $283.59   (present tax $2392.42-$2108.43 at assessment of $168,935)

7. Included exhibits are the property cards for properties in question

State Tax Form 135/135E   Notice of Refusal to Abate/Exempt
Property Tax

THE COMMON WEALTH OF MASSACHUSETTS
SWANSEA
OFFICE OF THE BOARD OF ASSESSORS

September 16, 2002

[Ferdinand & Claudia]
217 Main Drive
Swansea, MA 02777
[   ]

This notice informs you that your application dated June 11, 2002, for an abatement/exemption of the Fiscal Year 2002 Personal/Real Property Tax assessed as of January 1, 2001 to Ferdinand & Claudia has been denied under the provisions of Chapter 59 of the General Laws.

_____ Your application was denied by vote of the assessors on _____

__X__ Your application was deemed denied on _____September 11, 2002.
_____

You may appeal this denial in the manner and under the conditions provided by Chapter 59, Sections 64-65B of the General Laws.

Under those sections, your appeal may be made to the Appellate Tax Board or to the County Commissioners. The appeal must be filed within three months of the date your_application_was denied by vote of the assessors or within three months of the date your application was deemed denied, whichever is applicable. With certain exceptions, you must also pay at least one-half of the tax on personal property and, if the real property tax for the fiscal year is more than $2,000, all of the tax on real property without Incurring interest on any installment payment in order for the Appellate Tax Board or County Commissioners to hear the appeal.

If your application was denied by vote of the assessors, the assessors cannot take further action on your application unless you appeal their decision to the Appellate Tax Board or County Commissioners. However, if your application was deemed denied, the assessors may grant an abatement in final settlement of your application during the period for filing an appeal. If a settlement is not reached and an abatement not granted during that time, you must file a timely appeal for the assessors to be able to take any further action on your application.

Swansea, MA 02777	217 Main Drive Map 6 Lot 7-J	
Location of Property	Street and Number	Lot

Board of Assessors
of   SWANSEA

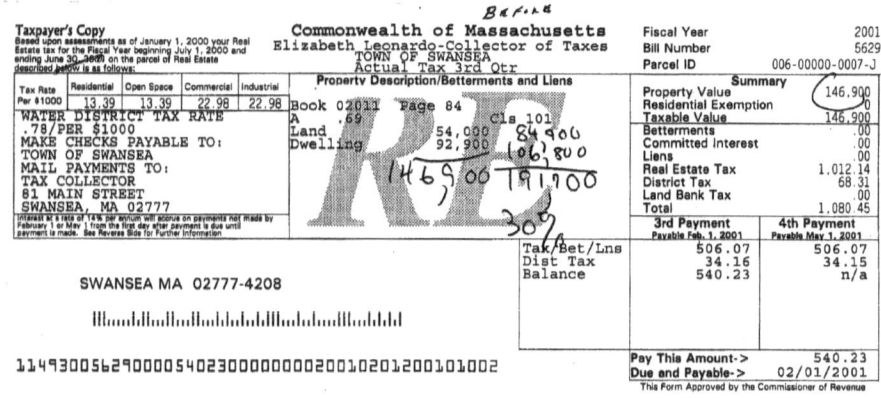

Message Area

ABATEMENT APPLICATIONS MUST BE RECEIVED IN THE ASSESSORS OFFICE BY FEBRUARY 1, 2001.

ANY QUESTIONS REGARDING THIS NEW BILLING FORMAT SHOULD BE DIRECTED TO THE TAX COLLECTOR'S OFFICE (508) 324-6701

PAYMENTS RECEIVED AFTER DECEMBER 22, 2000 ARE NOT REFLECTED ON THIS BILL. 3RD QUARTER PAYMENT IS DUE ON FEBRUARY 1, 2001.

INTEREST AT A RATE OF 14% PER ANNUM WILL ACCRUE ON PAYMENTS NOT MADE BY FEBRUARY 1, 2001 FROM THE FIRST DAY AFTER PAYMENT IS DUE UNTIL PAYMENT IS MADE. SEE REVERSE SIDE FOR FURTHER INFORMAITON.

Message Area

THIS IS THE FINAL BILL FOR FISCAL YEAR 2002.

PLEASE DIRECT QUESITIONS REGARDING THE BILL TO THE
TAX COLLECTOR'S OFFICE (508) 674-5730 MONDAY, TUESDAY, THURSDAY & FRIDAY
9:00 AM TO 4:00 PM AND WEDNESDAY 9:00 AM TO 5:00 PM.

QUESTIONS REGARDING PROPERTY VALUES SHOULD BE DIRECTED TO THE BOARD
OF ASSESSORS.

THE DUE DATE OF THIS BILL IS JULY 8, 2002

DEADLINE FOR ABATEMENT APPLICATIONS TO BE IN THE ASSWSSORS OFFICE IS
JULY 8, 2002

THE COMMONWEALTH OF MASSACHUSETTS
DEPARTMENT OF REVENUE
TAX RATE RECAPITULATION

of   FISCAL 2001

SWANSEA
City\Town\District

Dec 12, 2000

I. TAX RATE SUMMARY

Ia. Total amount to be raised (from IIe) $ 25,017,261.88

Ib. Total estimated receipts and other revenue sources (from IIIe)

$ 9,991,547.50

Ic. Tax levy (Ia minus Ib) $ 15,025,714.38

Id. Distribution of Tax Rates and levies

CLASS	(b) Levy Percentage (from LA-5)	(c) IC above times Each percent In col (b)	(d) Valuation By class (from LA-5)	(e) Tax Rates (c) / (d) x 1000	(f) Levy by class (d) x (e) / 1000
Residential	69.07989%	10,487,783.35	783,273,608	13.39	10,488,033.61
Exempt					
Open Space	0.0000%	0.00	0		
Commercial	24.8292%	3,730,764.67	162,339,592	22.98	3,730,563.82
Exempt					
Industrial	1.5943%	239,554.96	10,423,800	22.98	239,538.92
SUBTOTAL	96.2224%		956,037,000		14,458,136.35
Personal	3.7776%	567,911.39	24,698,783	22.98	567,578.03
TOTAL	100.0000%		980,735,783		15,025,714.38

Board of Assessors of   SWANSEA   12-4-00   508-324-6702
                         City or Town   Date   Tel. No.

Do Not Write Below This Line—For Department of Revenue Use Only

Reviewed By

Date _____ 12/19/00

Approved: _____ DEC 19, 2000

Director of Accounts

How to measure your house

Measure to nearest foot

<u>Correct Method</u>   <u>Incorrect Method</u>

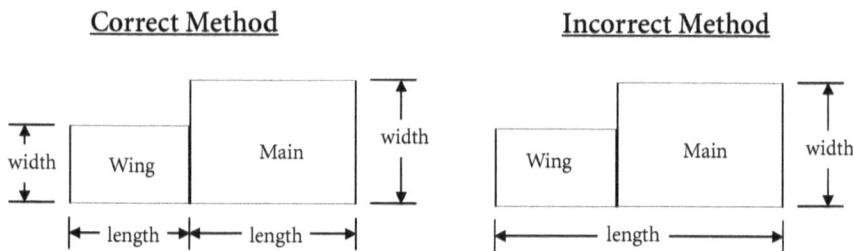

Measure wing only if it includes finished living space.

Do not measure wing if its sole purpose is a garage.

To insure an accurate cost replacement analysis of your home, measure ground floor dimensions as accurately as possible.

Note: THIS IS ONLY AN ILLUSTRATION

REAL ESTATE TAXES

ARE YOU OVERPAYING YOUR TAXES__ARE YOU OVERASSESSED

THIS THE "GRID" MENTIONED IN THE ARTICLE

AN EVALUATION OF YOUR "ASSESSED VALUE" AS COMPARED TO YUOR NEIGHBORS

ITEM	SUBJECT	COMPARABLE NO. 1		COMPARABLE NO. 2		COMPARABLE NO. 3	
		NEIGHBOR		NEIGHBOR		NEIGHBOR	
Address	ANYWHERE, USA	1/4 Mile		1/8 Mile		1/2 Mile	
Proximity to Subject							
VALUE ADJUSTMENTS	DESCRIPTION	DESCRIPTION	+(-) $ Adjustment	DESCRIPTION	+(-) $ Adjustment	DESCRIPTION	+(-) $ Adjustment
ASSESSED VALUE	ASSESSED		ASSESSED		ASSESSED		
110,000	Value	90,100	Value	109,000	Value	102,000	
Location	Average	Average	---	Average	---	Average	---
Site Sq. Ft.	8000	8500	---	12,000	-2000	16,000	-3000
View	Average	Average	---	Average	---	Average	---
Design and Appeal	Ranch	Ranch	---	Ranch	---	Ranch	---
Quality of Construction	Average	Average	---	Average	---	Average	---
Age	35	38	---	40	---	41	---
Condition	Good	Good	---	Good	---	Good	---
Above Grade	Total|Bdrms|Baths	Total|Bdrms|Baths		Total|Bdrms|Baths		Total|Bdrms|Baths	
Room Count	6|3|1.5	6|3|1.0	+500	6|3|2.0	-500	7|3|2.5	-1000
Gross Living Area	1200 Sq. Ft.	1100 Sq. Ft.	+2000	1300 Sq. Ft.	-2000	1400 Sq. Ft.	-4000
Basement & Finished Rooms Below Grade	100% 0 %	100% 90 %	-2000	100% 0 %	---	100% 90 %	-3000
Functional Utility	Good	Good	---	Good	---	Good	---
Heating/Cooling	Oil/None	Gas/None	---	Oil/None	---	Gas/None	---
Energy Efficient Items	Combos,Ins.	Combos, Ins.	---	Combos/Ins.	---	Combos/Ins.	---
Garage/Carport	1 Stall Det	No Garage	+8000	2 Stall G.	-4000	No Garage	+8000
Porch, Patio, Deck, Fireplace(s), etc.	No F/Place	1 F/place	-1500	No F/Place	---	1 F/Place	-1500
Fence, Pool, etc.	Above Gr.Pool	No Pool	+3000	In-Gr.Pool	---	Above GrP.	+3000
	Fence	No Fence	+300	Fence	---	No Fence	+300
Net Adj. (total)		[X] + [-] $10,300		[+] [X] [-] $ 8500		[ ] [+] [X] [-] $ 1200	
Adjusted Comparable		$ 100,400		$ 100,500		$ 100,800	

Comments : The Average of the three Comparables indicate an Assessed Value of the property at approximately $100.00 as the Assessed Value of your home. based on the Comparables above. IfyourTax Rate is for example $16.36 per Thousand of Assessed Value,then you are paying $16.36 times the overassessment of $10,000 (Your Assessed Value of $110.00 minus $100,00 equals $10,000 over-Assessment.) Then, $16.36 x 10=$163.36 overpayment in Taxes. This is only an

Gross Living Area Adjustment = $20 per sq. ft.   Illustration.

Note: The Assessed Value placed on your property is generally not the same as the Fatr Market Value, it is usually a ratio of the true Value. Ex. A home that would bring $ 150,000 if placed for sale ,called Fair Market Value, but Assessed at $75,000. has an Assessment Ratuo of 50 %.

If you beleive you are being overassessed,get a Market Analysis or an Appraisal. In the above example, an overassessment of $163 per year,results in $1633 in 10 years.

Buying A New Home?

In becoming a new homebuyer you need to know where and how to begin the home buying process. The following information should help you to determine whether you are ready to buy a new home.

You are probably ready to buy your own home if

1. You have a steady source of income and your current income is reliable.
2. You have money saved for a down payment.
3. You have a good record of paying your bills, and have few long-term debts, like car payments.
4. You have the ability to pay a mortgage every month, and any other additional costs.

The maximum loan amount is decided by the lender, by using a ratio where usually the monthly mortgage payments do not exceed 29% of gross income, and the mortgage payment, combined with Non-housing expenses does not exceed 41 % of income.

Examples:

gross annual income	gross monthly income	29% available for housing
$15,000	$1250	$363
$25,000	$2083	$604
$35,000	$2917	$846
$40,000	$3333	$967
$50,000	$4167	$1208

Be sure that you can meet the necessary requirements as stated above before proceeding any further. If you can, then continue with the guides in this section.

Determine Your Housing Needs

1. Makes a list of your priorities: location, size availability to public transportation, local schools, community resources and access to local facilities and amenities.
2. Obtain comparable listings of what homes are selling for in certain communities and neighborhoods by contacting a realtor who should have access to comparable sales maintained on a database.
3. Property taxes: Contact the local assessor's office. The previous year's taxes are usually included in the listing information. Tax rates can change from year to year, so these figures may be approximate.

Other Considerations

Are there enough bedrooms and bathrooms and is the house structurally sound? Be sure to check the mechanical systems and appliances and see if your furniture fits in the desired locations. If anything needs to be repaired or replaced will the seller repair or replace the items?

Before you buy, be sure to communicate often with your real estate agent about everything you are looking for. It will help avoid wasting your time.

Home Inspections

The lender usually requires a home inspection by a licensed home inspector. It is to your advantage to have a home inspection performed to make you aware of any repairs that are needed.

It is a good idea to have a home inspection before you sign a written offer since once the deal is closed, you have bought the house 'as is.' You may want to include an inspection clause in the offer when negotiating for a home. An inspection clause gives you an "out" on buying the house if serious problems are found, or gives you the ability to renegotiate the purchase price if repairs are needed. An inspection clause can also specify that the seller must fix the problem(s) before you purchase the house.

It is a good idea to be there for the inspection, though it is not required. The inspection is a good time to ask about general maintenance questions.

It is also a good idea to consider having your home inspected for the presence of a variety of health related risk factors, such as asbestos, radon gas, or possible problems with the water or waste disposal system.

Protecting Your Family From Lead In The Home

If the house you are considering was built before 1978 and you have children under the age of seven, you will want to have an inspection for lead based paint. It is important to know that lead flakes from paint can be present in both the home and in the soil surrounding the house. The problem can be fixed temporarily by repairing damaged paint surfaces or planting grass over affected soil. Hiring a lead abatement contractor to remove paint chips and seal damaged areas will fix the problem permanently.

Will I Need A Lawyer?

Laws vary by state. Some states require a lawyer to assist in several aspects of the home buying process, while others do not, as long as a qualified real estate professional is involved. You may want to hire a lawyer anyway to help with the complex paperwork and legal contracts, even if your state does not require one.

A lawyer can review contracts, make you aware of special considerations and assist you with the closing process. Perhaps your real estate agent may be able to recommend a lawyer. If not, shop around. Find out what services are provided for what fee, and if the attorney is experienced at representing homebuyers.

Homeowners Insurance And Costs

A paid homeowner's insurance policy (or a paid receipt for one) is required at closing, so arrangements will have to be made prior to that day. Be sure to shop around among several insurance companies. Consider the cost of insurance when you look at homes. Newer homes and homes constructed with materials like brick tend to have lower premiums. Avoid areas prone to natural disasters, like flooding. If your home is located in a flood plain, the lender will require that you have flood insurance before lending any money to you.

Making An Offer

Your real estate agent will assist you in making an offer, which will include the following information:

- Complete legal description of the property
- Amount of earnest money
- Down payment and financing details
- Proposed move-in date
- Price you are offering
- Proposed closing date
- Length of time the offer is valid
- Details of the deal

Keep in mind that a sale commitment depends on negotiating a satisfactory contract with the seller, not just making an offer.

Determining The Initial Offer

Calculating your offer should involve several factors:

- What homes are selling for in the area
- The condition of the home
- How long the home has been on the market
- Financing terms
- The seller's situation

Listen to your real estate agents advice, but follow your own instincts on deciding a fair price. By the time you are ready to make an offer, you should have a good idea of what the home is worth and what you can afford. Be prepared for give and take negotiation, which is very common when buying a home. The buyer and seller may often go back and forth until they can agree on a price.

Ernest money

Ernest money is money put down to demonstrate that you are serious about buying a home, and it must be substantial enough to demonstrate good faith. It is usually between 1 to 5 % of the purchase price, although the amount can vary with local customs and conditions. If your offer is accepted, the earnest money becomes part of your down payment or closing costs. If the offer is rejected, your money is returned to you. If you back out of a deal, you may forfeit the entire amount.

Home Warranties

Home warranties offer you protection for a specific period of time (usually one year), against potentially costly problems like unexpected repairs on appliances or home systems, which are not covered by homeowners insurance.

Mortgages

Generally speaking, a mortgage is a loan obtained to purchase real estate. The mortgage is a lien (a legal claim) on the home or property that secures the promise to pay the debt. All mortgages have two things in common: principal and interest.

Loan To Value Ratio

The loan to value ratio is the amount of money you borrow compared with the price or appraised value of the home that you are purchasing, with each loan having a specific loan to value limit. For example, with a 95% loan to value limit on a home priced at $100,000, you could borrow up to $95,000 (95% of $100,0000), and would have to pay $5,000 as a down payment. The loan to value ratio reflects the amount of equity that borrowers have in their homes.

The higher the loans to value ratio the less cash homebuyers are required to pay out of their own funds. So, to protect lenders against potential loss in case of default, loan to value ratios of 80% or more usually require a mortgage insurance policy.

Types Of Loans Available And Advantages Of Each

Fixed Rate Mortgages:
Payments remain the same for the life of the loan.
Types:

- 15 year and 30 year

Advantages:

- Predictable

- Housing costs remain unaffected by interest rate changes and inflation.

- In the first 23 years of the 30 year loan more interest is paid off than principal, meaning larger tax deductions. As inflation and costs of living increase, mortgage payments become a smaller part of overall expenses.

- A 15 year loan is usually made at a lower interest rate, and equity is built faster because early payments pay more principal.

Adjustable Rate Mortgages (ARMs)
Payments increase or decrease on a regular schedule with changes in interest rates, with increases subject to limits.
Types:

- Balloon mortgage, which offer very low rates for an initial period of time, usually 5, 7, or 10 years, when time has elapsed the balance is due or refinanced (though not automatically).

- Two step mortgage: the interest rate adjusts only once and remains the same for the life of the loan.

Adjustable rate mortgages are linked to a specific index or margin.
Advantages:

- Generally offer lower initial interest rates.

- Monthly payments can be lower.

- May allow borrower to qualify for a larger loan amount.

If you are confident that your income will increase steadily over the years or if you anticipate a move in the near future and are not concerned about potential increases in interest rates, then an adjustable rate mortgage may make sense to you.

Other General Information Regarding Loans

Prepayment

You can pay off your loan ahead of schedule by sending in extra money each month or making an extra payment at the end of the year, thus, accelerating the process of paying off the loan. When you send in the extra money, be sure to indicate that the excess payment is to be applied to the principal. Most lenders allow loan prepayments, although you may have to pay a prepayment penalty to do so. If your lender has prepayment penalties, you should seek another lender. When you first contact your lender, ask all the questions that you may have before you sign up or apply for the loan, so, that in case you are unhappy with some of the lender's conditions you may bow out before you are charged any fees.

First Time Homebuyer

There are special mortgages for first time homebuyers offered by some lenders with affordable mortgage options which can help first time homebuyers overcome obstacles that made purchasing a home more difficult in the past. Lenders may now be able to help borrowers who do not have a lot of money saved for the down payment and closing costs, have no credit or a poor credit history, have quite a bit of long term debt, or have experienced income irregularities.

Down payments

There are mortgage options now available that only require a down payment of 5% or less of the purchase price. But, the larger the down payment, the less you have to borrow, and the more equity you will have. Mortgages with less than a 20% down payment generally require a mortgage insurance policy to secure the loan. When considering the size of your down payment, consider that you will also need money for closing costs, moving expenses, possible repairs, and/or decorating.

Monthly Mortgage Payments

The monthly mortgage payment mainly pays off principal and interest. However, most lenders also include local real estate taxes, homeowners insurance, and mortgage insurance, if applicable.

Factors that affect mortgage payments are:

- The amount of the down payment
- The interest rate
- The length of the repayment term
- The payment schedule.

These will all affect the size of your mortgage payment.

Influence Of The Interest Rate Factor

A lower interest rate allows you to borrow more money than a high rate with the same monthly payment. Interest rates can fluctuate as you shop for a loan, so, ask lenders if they offer a "rate lock in " which guarantees a specific interest rate for a certain period of time.

A lender must disclose the annual percentage rate (APR) of a loan to you. The APR shows the cost of a mortgage loan by expressing it in terms of a yearly interest rate. It is generally higher than the interest rate because it also includes the cost of points, mortgage insurance and other fees included in the loan.

If you have a fixed rate loan and interest rates decrease significantly you may want to investigate refinancing. It is generally agreed by most professionals that if you plan to be in your home for at least 18 months and you can get a rate 2% less than your current one, refinancing is the wise thing to do. However, refinancing may involve paying many of the same fees paid at the original closing, plus origination and application fees.

Discount Points

Discount points allow you to lower your interest rate, and are essentially pre-paid interest, with each point equaling the total loan amount. Generally, for each point paid on a 30 year mortgage, the interest rate is reduced by 1/8 or 0.125 of a percentage point. When shopping for loans, ask lenders for an interest rate with 0 points and then see how much the rate decreases with each point paid. Discount points are smart if you plan to stay in the home for some time, since they can lower the monthly payment. Points are tax deductible when you purchase a home and you may be able to negotiate for the seller to pay for some of them.

Escrow Accounts

An escrow account is established by your lender and is a place to set aside a portion of your monthly mortgage payment to cover annual charges for home owners insurance, mortgage insurance, (if applicable) and property taxes. Escrow accounts are a good idea because they assure money will always be available for these payments. If you use an escrow account to pay property taxes or homeowner's insurance, be sure you are not penalized for late property tax or home insurance payments, since it is the lenders responsibility to make those payments.

Steps Taken To Secure A Loan

The first step in securing a loan is to complete a loan application. You will need the following information:

- Pay stubs for the past 2 to 3 months
- W2 forms for the past 2 years
- Recent bank statements
- Tax returns for the past 2 years
- Information on long term debts
- Proof of any other income
- Address and description of the property that you wish to buy
- Sales contract

During the application process, the lender will order a report on your credit history and a professional appraisal of the property that you want to purchase. The application process usually takes between one to six weeks.

Choosing The Right Lender

Be careful in choosing your lender. Look for financial stability and a reputation for customer satisfaction. Be sure to choose a company that gives helpful advice and that makes you comfortable. A lender that has the authority to approve and process your loan locally is preferable, since it will be easier for you to monitor the status of your application and ask questions. Also, it is beneficial when the lender knows home values and conditions in the local area. Do research and ask family, friends, and your real estate agent for recommendations.

Pre Qualifying And Pre Approval

Pre qualification is an informal way to see how much you may be able to borrow. You can be 'pre qualified' over the phone, without any obligation or paperwork, by telling a lender your income, your long-term debts, and how large a down payment you can afford. This helps you arrive at a ballpark figure of the amount you may have available to spend on a house-

Pre approval is a lender's actual commitment to lend to you. It involves assembling the financial records necessary (without the property description and sales contract) and going through a preliminary approval process. Pre approval gives you a definite idea of what you can afford and shows sellers that are serious about the purchase.

Choosing The Best Loan Program

Your personal situation will determine the best kind of loan for you. You can help narrow down your search among the many options available and discover which loan suits you best.

Examples:
- Do you expect your finances to change over the next few years?
- Are you planning to live in this home for a long period of time?
- Do you wish to be free of mortgage debt as your children approach college age or as you prepare for retirement?

Your Credit History And Information Sources

There are three major credit reporting companies: Equifax, Experian, and Transunion.

Obtaining your credit report is as easy as calling and requesting one. Once you receive your report, it is important to verify its accuracy. Double-check the high credit limit, total amount, and past due columns. It is a good idea to get copies from all three companies to assure there are no mistakes, since any of the three could be providing a report to your lender.

Fees ranging from $5 to $20 are usually charged to issue credit reports, but some states permit citizens to acquire a free one. Contact the reporting companies at the numbers listed below for more information:

Credit Reporting Company	Phone Number
Experian	1-800-682-7654
Equifax	1-800-685-1111
Transunion	1-800-916-8800

If you find a mistake in your credit history, write to the reporting company, pointing out the error, and provide proof of the mistake. You can also request to have your own comments added to explain problems. For example, if you made a late payment, due to illness, explain that for the record. Lenders are usually understanding about legitimate problems.

Credit Bureau Scores

A credit bureau score is a number, based upon your credit history, that represents the possibility that you will be unable to repay a loan. Lenders use it to determine your ability to qualify for a mortgage loan. The better the score, the better your chances are of getting a loan. You can work to keep your score acceptable by maintaining a good credit history, by paying your bills on time and not overextending yourself by buying more than you can afford. For details, ask your lender.

Compare Loan Terms Between Lenders

Devise a check list for the information from each lending institution. Include the following:
- Company's name and basic information
- Type of mortgage
- Minimum down payment required
- Interest rate and points
- Closing costs

- Loan processing time
- Whether prepayment is allowed

Be sure to call every lender on your list on the same day, as interest rates fluctuate daily. In addition to your research, your real estate agent may have access to a data base of lender and mortgage options.

The Loan Origination Process

There are costs associated with the loan origination process. When you turn in your application, you will be required to pay a loan application fee to cover the costs of underwriting the loan. This fee pays for the home appraisal, a copy of your credit report. and any additional charges that may be necessary. The application fee is generally nonrefundable.

Real Estate Settlement Procedures Act (RESPA)

This act requires lenders to disclose information to potential customers throughout the mortgage process, and by doing so, it protects borrowers from abuses by lending institutions. RESPA mandates that lenders fully inform borrowers about all closing costs, lender servicing and escrow account practices.

Good Faith Estimate

A good faith estimate is an estimate that lists all fees paid before closing costs, and any escrow costs that you will encounter when purchasing a home. The lender must supply it within three days of your application so that you can make accurate judgements when shopping for a loan.

Steps To Follow During The Lending Process

To ensure that you will not fall victim to loan fraud, be sure to follow all of these steps as you apply for a loan:

- Refuse to sign any blank documents.
- Be sure to read and understand everything before you sign.

- Do not buy property for anyone else.
- Do not overstate your income.
- Do not overstate how long you have been employed.
- Do not overstate your assets.
- Accurately report your debts.
- Do not change your income tax returns for any reason.
- Tell the whole truth about gifts.
- Do not list fake co-borrowers on your loan application.
- Be truthful about your credit problems, past and present.
- Be honest about your intention to occupy the house.
- Do not provide false supporting documents.

After you have applied for a loan, it usually takes a lender one to six weeks to complete the evaluation of your application. Sometimes, a lender will ask for more information after the application has been submitted. Once all the information has been verified, the lender will call you to let you know the outcome of your application. If your loan is approved, a closing date is set up, and the lender will review the closing process with you. After closing, you will be able to move into your new home.

The Final Walk Through Before Closing

If possible, examine the house without the furniture, giving you a clear view of everything. Check the walls and ceiling carefully, as well as any work that the seller agreed to do in response to the inspection. Any problems discovered previously that you find uncorrected should be brought up prior to closing. It is the seller's responsibility to fix them.

Closing Costs

Closing costs usually consist of the following:
- Property taxes, to cover tax period to date
- Attorney's or escrow fees (yours and your lenders, if applicable)

- Interest paid from the date of the closing to 30 days before the first monthly payment.
- Loan origination fee (covers lenders administrative costs).
- Recording fees
- Survey fee.
- First premium of mortgage insurance (if applicable)
- Title insurance (yours and your lenders)
- Loan discount points.
- First payment to escrow account for future real estate
- Taxes and insurance
- Paid receipt for homeowner's insurance policy (and fire and flood insurance if applicable)
- Any documentation preparation fee.

On Closing Day

On closing day you will present your paid homeowner's insurance policy or a binder and receipt showing that the premium has been paid. The closing agent will then list the money you owe the seller (remainder of down payment, prepaid taxes, etc.) and then the money the seller owes you (unpaid taxes and prepaid rent, if applicable). The seller will provide proof of any inspection, warranties, etc.

Once you are sure you understand all the documentation, you will sign the mortgage, agreeing that if you don't make the payments, the lender is entitled to sell your property and apply the sale price against the amount you owe plus expenses. You will also sign a mortgage note, promising to repay the loan. The seller will give you the title to the house in the form of a signed deed.

You will pay the lender's agent all closing costs and, in turn, he or she will provide you with a settlement statement of all the items for which you have paid. The deed and the mortgage will then be recorded in the state registry of deeds, and you will be a homeowner.

What you get at closing:

- Settlement statement (itemizes services provided and the fees charged. It is filled out by the closing agent and must be given to you at or before closing).
- Truth-in-lending statement
- Mortgage note
- Mortgage or deed of trust
- Binding sales contract prepared by the seller (Your lawyer should review it.)
- The keys to your new home.

Down Payments And Private Mortgage Insurance (PMI)

Some lenders require 20% of the home's purchase price as a down payment. However, many lenders now offer loans that require less than 20% down, sometimes as little as 5% down on conventional loans. If a 20% down payment is not made, lenders usually require the homebuyer to purchase private mortgage insurance (PMI) to protect the lender in case the homebuyer fails to pay. When government assisted programs such as the federal housing administration (FHA), Veterans administration (VA), or rural development services are available, the down payment requirements may be substantially smaller.

Questions to ask:

- What are the lender's requirements for a down payment?
- What do you need to do to verify that funds for your down payment are available?
- Does the lender offer any special programs?
- Is a PMI required for your loan?
- What will be the total cost of the insurance?
- How long you will be required to carry the PMI?

Note: When you have reached the point where you have at least 20% of the home's present value in equity, you should ask that the monthly private mortgage insurance payments (PMI) be cancelled. But to qualify for cancellation of your PMI you will have to demonstrate to the lender that your property has increased in value (due to inflation). If you want to cancel your PMI success-fully, contact the lender to whom you send payments every month. Ask the lender to order an appraisal to establish market value.

Average appreciation of home values nationwide has increased dramatically. People who pay private mortgage insurance premiums are moving far faster than anticipated toward the magic point of 20% equity, where they can legally request cancellation of monthly premiums by their lender.

Though many homeowners remain unaware of their rights under Federal mortgage insurance cancellation legislation that took effect in July 2000, they may be qualified-now to request termination of their premium payments. Under the law, borrowers whose equity stakes in their homes reach 20% may be eligible to ask their lender to dispense with mortgage insurance coverage.

Lenders on homes where the borrower's down payment is less than 20 percent generally require private mortgage insurance (PMI). The coverage is almost always paid for by the borrower, but protects the lender against loss in the event of the borrower's default or a foreclosure.

About one million homebuyers nationwide take out mortgages with PMI coverage every year. Typically the premiums add $40 to $100 dollars a month to the cost of the loan. The large investors Fannie Mae and Freddie Mac buy an estimated 75% to 80% of those PMI covered loans. Both companies have directed lenders who service their loans to consider canceling PMI coverage at the borrower's request when the borrower can demonstrate that he or she has exceeded the 20% equity point, and has maintained a good payment history.

Appreciation Rate

The recent torrid appreciation rate in home resale values has dramatically compressed the time span necessary for a low down payment borrower to reach the 20 percent equity mark. A purchaser of a $100,000 townhouse two years ago could be much closer to the cancellation request point than he or she might have imagined.

For example, assume the buyer put down a 10% down payment, received a $90,000, 30 year fixed rate loan at 7½ % and has experienced a 6% annual appreciation. Thanks to inflation and a small amount of pay down on the loan principal, that buyer could hit the premium cancellation request point before the end of the third year of ownership. This underscores the need for anyone paying PMI premiums to be familiar with the timing and procedures for requesting cancellation of their loan insurance. This can be a little tricky.

Here's what you need to know:

If your loan closed before last July 29th, your lender does not have to cancel PMI at your request unless it, or the owner of the loan, has a standard policy of doing so. Most major lenders and investors do have this policy, and they should spell out the procedures in a disclosure once a year. Since the odds are strong that your loan is owned by either Freddie Mac or Fannie Mae, the company servicing of your loan will have to consider any bona fide request for cancellation at or above the 20% equity point. What constitutes bona fide? To begin with, you need to have a solid payment history.

A Solid Payment History

You need to have a solid payment history. Fannie Mae and Freddie Mac standards are identical: No 30 day late mortgage payments in the last 12 months and no 60 day late payments in the last 24 months. If you pass the payment purity test, there is another test you must pass. You have to be able to show that your home's value has increased sufficiently to give you an equity stake of 20 percent or more.

You may require more than 29 percent if your loan closed less than 5 years ago and you have not made substantial improvements to the property, i.e., you are basing your case on rapid appreciation alone. Both Fannie Mae and Freddie Mac both require a 25 percent equity stake for PMI cancellation. For loans more than 5 years old, the 29 percent equity standard is acceptable to both.

How do you know when you are even close to the required home level? You have got to use at least one of the several valuation methods: a low cost "appraisal consultation", a "broker price opinion"(BPO), an on line "automated valuation model" (AVM), or a full-scale appraisal. Your lender will discuss these with you and tell you which one that they will accept.

Do not hire an appraiser on your own. Be sure that the appraisal that you select is acceptable to the lender.

Government Assisted Programs

The most widely used government programs to help the homebuyer are HUD-FHA loans and VA (veterans' affairs) loans.

FHA Loans

The FHA (Federal Housing Administration) is an agency within HUD (United States Department of Housing and Urban Development). The FHA provides private lenders with mortgage insurance, giving them the security they need to lend to first time buyers who might not be able to qualify for conventional loans. The FHA has helped more than 26 million Americans buy a home.

FHA Assistance

The FHA works to make homeownership a possibility for more Americans. With the FHA, you do not need perfect credit or a high paying job to qualify for a loan. The FHA also makes loans more accessible by requiring smaller down payments than conventional loans. In fact, an FHA down payment could be as little as a few months rent.

FHA is funded by premiums paid by FHA insured loan borrowers. No tax dollars are used to fund the program. Lender claims, paid by the FHA mortgage insurance program, are drawn from this mutual mortgage insurance fund.

FHA loan limits vary throughout the country, from $115,200 in low cost areas to $208,800 in high cost areas. The loan limits for multi unit homes are higher than those for single units, and also vary by area. Because these maximums are linked to the conforming loan limit and average area home prices, FHA loan limits are periodically subject to change. Ask your lender for details and confirmation of current limits.

Steps Involved In The FHA Loan Process

The FHA loan application process is similar to that of a conventional loan. With the exception of a few additional forms with the new automation measure, FHA loans may be originated more quickly than before. And, if you do not prefer a face to face meeting, you can apply for a FHA loan via mail, telephone, the Internet, or videoconference.

Income Needed To Qualify For An FHA Loan

There is no minimum income requirement to qualify for a FHA loan, but you must prove steady income for at least three years, and demonstrate that you have consistently paid your bills on time. Income type is not as important as income steadiness with the FHA. You can carry short term debt, as long as it can be paid off within 10 months: Also, some regular expenses, like child care are not considered debt. Ask your lender or real estate agent about meeting the FHA debt to income ratio.

The Debt To Income Ratio For FHA Loans

The FHA allows you to use 29% of your income towards housing costs and 41% towards housing expenses and other long-term debt. With a conventional loan the qualifying ratio allows only 28% toward housing and 36% towards housing and other debt. You can exceed this ratio if you have the following:

- A large down payment
- A demonstrated ability to pay more toward your housing expenses
- Substantial cash reserves
- Net worth enough to repay the mortgage regardless of income
- Evidence of acceptable credit history or limited credit use
- Less than maximum mortgage terms
- Funds provided by an organization
- A decrease in monthly housing expenses

Down Payment

You must have a down payment of at least 3% of the purchase price of the home. Most affordable loan programs offered by private lenders require between a 3% to 5% down payment, with a minimum of 3% coming directly from the borrower's own funds. Besides your own funds you may use cash gifts or money from a private savings club. If you can do certain repairs and improvements yourself, your labor may be used as part of a down payment (called sweat equity). If you are doing a lease purchase, paying extra rent to the seller may also be considered the same as accumulating cash.

Credit History

The FHA is more flexible than conventional lenders in its qualifying guidelines. In fact, the FHA allows you to re establish credit if:

- Two years have passed since a bankruptcy has been discharged
- All judgements have been paid
- Any outstanding tax liens have been satisfied or appropriate arrangements have been made to establish a repayment plan with the IRS or state department of revenue.
- Three years have passed since a foreclosure or a deed in lieu has been resolved.

Without A Credit History?

If you are too young to have established credit, or you prefer to pay debts in cash there are other ways to prove your eligibility. Talk to your lender for details.

Closing Costs Associated With A FHA Loan

Except for the addition of a FHA mortgage insurance premium, FHA closing costs are similar to those of a conventional loan. The FHA requires a single, up front mortgage insurance premium equal to 2.25% of the mortgage to be paid at closing, or 1.75% if you complete the help program. This initial premium may be partly refunded if the loan is paid in full during he first seven years of the loan term. After closing, you will then be responsible for an annual premium, paid in monthly installments, if your mortgage is over 15 years or if you have a 15 year loan with a loan to value (LTV) greater than 90%. To learn how to receive a discount on the FHA initial mortgage premium, ask your real estate agent or lender for information on the Home buying Education Learning Program (HELP) from the FHA.

Although you cannot include your closing costs into your FHA loan, you may be able to use the amount you pay for them to help satisfy the down payment requirements. Ask your lender for details.

If you are buying a home, you can assume an existing FHA loan from the seller. Also, if you are selling your home, you many allow a buyer to assume your existing FHA loan. Assuming a loan can be very beneficial, since the process is streamlined and less expensive compared to that for a new loan. Also, assuming a loan can often result in a lower interest rate. The application process consists basically of a credit check and no property appraisal is required. You must demonstrate that you have enough income to support the mortgage loan. In this way, qualifying to assume a loan is similar to the qualification requirements for a new loan.

Options If You Fall Behind On Your Loan Payments

Call or write to your lender as soon as possible. Clearly explain the situation and be prepared to provide him or her with financial information. Talk to your lender or a HUD approved counseling agency for details. Here are a few options that may help you get back on track.

For FHA Loans:
- Keep living in your home to qualify for assistance
- Contact a HUD approved housing counseling agency (1-800-569-4287 or 1-800-877-83390)
- Cooperate with the counselor/lender trying to help you
- HUD has a number of special loss mitigation programs available to help you.

Special Forbearance:
- Your lender will arrange for a revised repayment plan which may include temporary reduction or suspension of payments
- You can qualify by having an involuntary reduction in your income or increase in living expenses.

Mortgage Modification :
- Allows you to refinance debt and/or extend the term of the mortgage loan, which may reduce your monthly payments

- You can qualify if you have recovered from financial problems, but your net income is less than before.

Partial Claim:
- Your lender may be able to help you obtain an interest free loan from HUD to bring your mortgage current.

Pre Foreclosure Sale:
- Allows you to sell your property and pay off your mortgage loan to avoid foreclosure.

Deed In Lieu Of Foreclosure:
- Enables you to voluntarily "give back" your property to the lender
- This will not let you keep your house, but it will help you avoid the costs, time, and effort of the foreclosure process

If you are having difficulty with an uncooperative lender or feel your loan source is not providing you with the most effective loss mitigation options, call the FHA loss mitigation center at 1-888-297-8685.

For Conventional Loans:

Talk to your lender about specific loss mitigation options. Work directly with him or her to request a "workout pocket". A secondary lender, like Fannie Mae or Freddie Mac, may have purchased your loan. Your lender can follow the appropriate guidelines set by Fannie Mae or Freddie Mac to determine the best option for your situation.

Fannie Mae does not deal directly with the borrower, they work with the lender to determine the loss mitigation program that best fits your needs. Freddie Mac, like Fannie Mae, will usually only work with the loan provider. However, if you encounter problems with your lender during the loss mitigation process, you can call customer service for help at 1-800-373-3343.

In any loss mitigation situation, it is important to remember a few helpful hints:

- Explore every reasonable alternative to avoid losing your home, but beware of scams.
- Watch out for equity skimming where a buyer offers to repay the mortgage or sell the property if you sign over the deed and move out.
- Watch out for phony counseling agencies that offer counseling for a fee, when it is often given at no charge.
- Don't sign anything that you don't understand

Mortgage Insurance

Mortgage insurance is a policy that protects lenders against some or most of the losses that result from defaults on home mortgages. It is required primarily for borrowers making a down payment of less than 20% of the purchase price of the home. Like home or auto insurance, mortgage insurance requires payment of a premium, is for protection against loss, and is used in the event of an emergency. If a borrower can not repay an insured mortgage loan as agreed, the lender may foreclose on the property and file a claim with the mortgage insurer for some or most of the losses. You need mortgage insurance only if you plan to make a down payment of less than 20 % of the purchase price of the home.

Private Mortgage Insurance (PMI)

PMI stands for private mortgage insurance or insurer. These are privately owned companies that provide mortgage insurance. They offer both standard and special affordable programs for borrowers. These companies provide guidelines to lenders that detail the types of loans they will insure. Lenders use these guidelines to determine borrower eligibility. Private Mortgage Insurers usually have stricter qualifying ratios and larger down payment requirements than the FHA, but their premiums are often lower and they insure loans that exceed the FHA limit.

203 (b) Loans

This is the most commonly used FHA program. It offers a low down payment, flexible qualifying guidelines, limited lender's fees, and a maximum loan amount.

203 (k) Loans

This is a loan that enables the homebuyer to finance both the purchase and rehabilitation of a home through a single mortgage. A portion of the loan is used to pay off the seller's existing mortgage and the remainder is placed in an escrow account and released as rehabilitation is completed.

Basic guidelines for 203 (k) loans are as follows:

- The home must be at least one year old.
- The cost of rehabilitation must be at least $5,000, but the total property value, including the cost of repairs, must fall within the FHA maximum mortgage limit.
- The 203 (k) loan must follow many of the 203 (b) eligibility requirements.

Talk to your lender about specific improvements, energy efficiency, and structural guidelines.

Energy Efficient Mortgage (EEM)

The energy efficient mortgage allows a homebuyer to save future money on utility bills. This is done by financing the cost of adding energy efficiency features to a new or existing home as part of a FHA insured home purchase. The EEM can be used with both 203 (b) and 203 (k) loans.

Basic guidelines for EEMs are as follows:

- The cost of improvements must be determined by a home energy rating system or by an energy consultant.
- This cost must be less than the anticipated savings from the improvements.

- One and two-unit, new or existing homes are eligible, condominiums are not.
- The improvements financed may be 5% of property value or $4,000, whichever is greater.
- The total must fall within the FHA loan limit.

FHA Bridal Registry Program

The bridal registry program allows couples to register with a lender and open up an interest bearing account, just as you might register at a department store for wedding gifts. Family and friends can deposit wedding gifts of cash into this account. These gifts can then be applied toward a down payment on a home.

Ask your lender for details.

Title I Loan

A Title I loan is used to make non-luxury renovations and repairs to a home. It is given by a lender and insured by FHA. It offers a manageable interest rate and repayment schedule. Loans are limited to between $5,000 and $20,000. If the loan amount is under $7,500, no lien is required against your home.

Ask your lender for details.

Other FHA Loans

FHA also insures loans for the purchase or rehabilitation or manufactured housing, condominiums, and cooperatives. It also has special programs for urban areas, disaster victims and members of the armed forces. Insurance from adjustable rate mortgages (ARMs) is also available from the FHA.

How To Obtain A FHA Insured Loan

Contact a FHA-approved lender such as a participating mortgage company, bank, savings and loan association, or thrift. For more information on the FHA and how you can, obtain a FHA loan, visit the HUD web site at http/www.hud.gov or call a HUD approved counseling agency at 1-800-569-4287 or 1-800-877-8339. You can contact HUD by visiting the web site at http/www.hud.gov or looking in the phone book "blue pages" for a listing of the HUD office near you.

Veterans Administration (VA) Loans

These loans are made only to qualified veterans of previous wars and require no down payment. Conditions are otherwise similar to FHA loans. Contact your real estate agent, broker, or local bank for detailed information.

Federal Benefits for Veterans and Dependents

Home Loan Guaranties

VA loan guarantees are made to service members, veterans, reservists and unremarried surviving spouses for the purchase of homes, condominiums and manufactured homes and for refinancing loans. VA guarantees part of the total loan, permitting the purchaser to obtain a mortgage with a competitive interest rate, even without a down payment if the lender agrees. VA requires that a down payment be made for the purchase of a manufactured home. VA also requires a down payment for a home or condominium if the purchase price exceeds the reasonable value of the property or the loan has a graduated payment feature. With a VA guarantee, the lender is protected against loss up to the amount of the guarantee if the borrower fails to repay the loan. A VA loan guarantee can be used to:

1. Buy a home
2. Buy a residential condominium
3. Build a home
4. Repair, alter or improve a home
5. Refinance an existing home loan
6. Buy a manufactured home with or without a lot

7. Buy and improve a manufactured home lot

8. Install a solar heating or cooling system or other weatherization improvements.

9. Purchase and improve a home simultaneously with energy efficient improvements.

10. Refinance an existing VA loan to reduce the interest rate and make energy-efficient improvements.

11. Refinance a manufactured home loan to acquire a lot.

Eligibility

Applicants must have a good credit rating, have an income sufficient to support mortgage payments, and agree to live in the property. To obtain a VA certificate of eligibility you must complete VA Form 26-1880, "Request for Determination of Eligibility and Available Loan Guaranty Entitlement," and submit it to the nearest VA regional office. http://www.va.gov/forms has links to Form 26-1880 and other VA forms. Eligibility varies with service.

World War II: (1) active duty service after Sept. 15, 1940, and prior to July 26, 1947; (2) discharge under other than dishonorable conditions; and (3) at least 90 days service unless discharged early for service-connected disability.

Post-World War II: (1) active duty service after July 25, 1947, and prior to June 27, 1950; (2) discharge under other than dishonorable conditions; and (3) 181 continuous days active duty unless discharged early for service-connected disability.

Korean Conflict: (1) active duty after June 26, 1950, and prior to Feb. 1, 1955; (2) discharge under other than dishonorable conditions; and (3) at least 90 days total service, unless discharged early for a service-connected disability.

Post Korean Conflict: (1) active duty between Jan. 31, 1955, and Aug. 5, 1964; (2) discharge under conditions other than dishonorable; (3) 181 days continuous service, unless discharged early for service-connected disability.

Borrower Beware: You Need To Know Your Rights

Do you really know your federally guaranteed legal rights vis-a-vis your lender? Did you know that if you complain to your mortgage company in any manner other than prescribed by federal law, you could lose some important federal consumer protections? And do you know how much time your lender or loan service has to get back to you and then solve your problem?

If these questions are drawing blanks, join the crowd. Federal officials familiar with mortgage borrower protections say only a tiny fraction of consumers have a grasp of their legal rights when disputes arise To make certain you've got the facts when you need them, here's a quick overview:

Mortgage complaints: If you have a serious problem with your lender or service's handling of your loan, you need to describe it in writing, not simply over the telephone. You need to send your written request along with your loan account number, to the complaint address provided by your lender at least once a year; Your letter should be separate from your monthly payment or other correspondence.

Action-response deadlines: Provided you have sent your complaint in this form, your lender is covered by key legal deadlines. Within 20 business days of receipt your lender must respond to you, at least acknowledging receipt of the letter and promising action. Within 60 business days, your lender must "correct or clarify" the problem itself.

Escrow accounts: The most common source of friction between homeowners and mortgage lenders is escrow accounts. Say, for instance, you question the way your escrow items have been calculated by the lender. You can telephone the lender's customer service number to talk about it. But if you don't like the answer you get, or you get no action or resolution, the only way to ensure coverage under the federal 20/60 day consumer protection rules is for you to send a formal written request, including your account number.

If your argument with the lender or service involves allegation of unpaid or overdue funds, invoking the 20/60-day rule can give you an added blanket of protection. During the 60 business-day period beginning with the lender's receipt of your qualified written request, the company is prohibited by federal law from informing credit bureaus about your alleged nonpayment. If you're not covered by the rule, on the other hand, your lender is free to tell the national credit bureaus, and through them, anyone checking on your credit, that you're delinquent on your mortgage payments. Even if it turns out later that you weren't.

Servicing transfers: This is another constant source of friction between lenders and their customers. Lenders frequently sell or transfer the rights to service your loan to other mortgage companies. But you are protected by federal law against surprise transfers or sales of your loan files and account. You are entitled to advance, written notice of any transfer. Your lender, in other words, cannot simply write or call you tomorrow and say, "we sold your mortgage to Tasmania Mortgage.com last week. Send all your future payments to Tasmania from now on, not to us. Have a good day."

No way. You must receive formal, federally prescribed notifications in writing from both your current lender and the new firm that will be handling the mortgage. The latest date you as a homeowner can be informed of a servicing transfer is 15 days before the date that the successor firm is scheduled to take over administration of the loan. The advance notification must give you the name, address, and toll-free servicing information number of the new firm.

No later than 15 days after the transfer occurs, the new service provider must contact you in writing and establish procedures for the new relationship. But here's a key consumer protection you've got: During the initial 60 days after your loan servicing account has been transferred, you may not be hit with late penalties for any mortgage payment you send on time to the first service provider, rather than to the new firm. You are held harmless for the innocent mistake of being confused about where to send your payments.

Of course, if your mistake is not innocent, and you sent your payment in late to the wrong place, don't look to federal law to protect you from lender penalties. You owe the money, 60-day rule or not.

Financial Guide

Your real estate investment is one of the most major buying decisions of your lifetime. This financial program will detail your realistic buying potential, as well as monthly home ownership costs for months to come. The following financial guide will clarify such questions as: What is your price range realistically in relation to purchasing your first home, townhouse, or condominium? Can you now afford to own a home as opposed to paying rent? Is now a good time to make a move upward? By completing the guide below, you can qualify your real estate goals.

The first key of successful house hunting is to establish a comfortable and confident relationship with the real estate company of your choice. You should be able to find many professional real estate offices to choose from.

The second major element of your real estate investment is selecting the proper route of financing your acquisition. Today's banks and lending institutions' rates and services are very competitive. Various mortgage plans are readily available in the market at the present time.

Before you decide how, where, and how much to finance, relax, sit down for an hour and qualify your specific financial outlook at the present time. Use a pencil, because certain figures may change between now and the closing date. PLAN YOUR FINANCIAL WORK, THEN WORK YOUR FINANCIAL PLAN.

SECTION #1   List All Available Assests

a. cash   _____
b. checking accounts   _____
                          _____
                          _____
c. savings accounts   _____
                          _____
                          _____

d. equity if present home (if applicable)   _____

e. tax returns   _____

f. bonds   _____

g. security deposits   _____

h. pre-paid rent   _____

i. insurance policies   _____

j. gifts   _____

k. miscellaneous   _____

Total Assets Realistically Obtainable   _____

SECTION #2   Estimated Settlement Costs

a. down payment   5%   _____

     10%   _____

     15%   _____

     20%   _____

     25%   _____

b. loan origination (points)   _____

c. appraisal fees   _____

d. credit report   _____

e. legal fees   _____

f. prepaid interest   _____

g. recording fees   _____

h. mortgage insurance premium   _____

i. lender's title insurance   _____

j. survey   _____

k. municipal lien certificate   _____

l. local real estate tax   _____

m. home inspection   _____

n. termite inspection   _____

o. taxes (escrow)   _____

p. other   _____

Estimated Initial Settlement Costs   _____

If the total of section #2 is larger than that of section #1, you may want to consider such alternatives as a lower down payment. Procedures vary with different types of mortgage loans, your real estate agent will assist you in comparisons.

SECTION #3 Monthly Income Analysis

a. gross monthly income of husband _____

b. gross monthly income of wife _____

c. rental income _____

d. stock dividends _____

e. other sources _____

Total Gross Monthly Income _____

SECTION #4

At this point of the program, you know what are your available assets, projected closing costs, and approximate amount of monthly income from all sources combined. By subtracting the total of estimated down payment from the anticipated purchase price of the property, you will know the amount of capital needed for our mortgage. Apply that figure to the mortgage loan calculator below to identify monthly principal and interest per $1,000.

MONTHLY LOAN CALCULATOR
Monthly Interest And Principal Per $1,000

Interest Rate	15 Years	20 Years	25 Years	30 Years
8%	9.56	8.36	7.72	7.34
9%	10.14	9.00	8.39	8.05
9½%	10.44	9.32	8.74	8.41
10%	10.75	9.65	9.09	8.78
10½%	11.06	9.99	9.45	9.15
11%	11.37	10.33	9.81	9.53
11½%	11.69	10.67	10.17	9.91
12%	12.01	11.02	10.54	10.29
12½%	12.33	11.37	10.91	10.68
13%	12.66	11.72	11.28	11.07
13½%	12.99	12.08	11.66	11.46
14%	13.32	12.44	12.04	11.85

Example: $95,500 mortgage @ 10% for 30 years=
95.5 x 8.78=838.49 per month plus taxes, insurance, etc.

By completing the previous sections, your financial picture should be relatively clear. Upon calculating the estimated mortgage payments versus your monthly income, you will qualify yourself for your real estate investment needs. The next section will outline the approximate monthly costs of ownership.

SECTION #5   Estimated Monthly Costs Of Home And Personal Obligations

a. private mortgage insurance (PMI)   _____
b. homeowner's insurance   _____
c. electricity   _____
d. heating fuel   _____
e. gas or propane   _____
f. sewerage   _____
g. sanitation control   _____
h. applicable taxes   _____
i. personal loans   _____
j. automobile loans   _____
k. health insurance   _____
l. life insurance   _____
m. child support   _____
n. alimony   _____
o. revolving credit   _____
p. common charges (condominiums only)   _____
q. miscellaneous   _____

Total Estimate Of Monthly Home And Personal Obligations
_____

By the end of Step #5, you are now aware of what your closing costs are, approximate monthly liabilities, down payment, total available assets, gross monthly income, as well as the basic monthly mortgage payments. The next step is to apply the above mentioned figures into a simplified outline:

AVAILABLE ASSETS   _____
CLOSING COSTS   _____
MONTHLY INCOME   _____

MONTHLY MORTGAGE   _____
   (principal, interest, taxes, PMI, homeowner's insurance and common charges)
MONTHLY OBLIGATIONS   _____

Generally, the monthly mortgage payment should not exceed 25-28% of your gross monthly income. And, your total monthly obligations, including your monthly mortgage payment, should not exceed 33-36% of your gross monthly income. Your real estate office will assist you in direction and decision making. You are making a major investment; do it wisely and successfully!

Protect Credit Cards From Fraud By Taking These Three Steps

If you suspect your card has been stolen:

1. Contact the fraud units at all three credit bureaus and ask them to puts fraud alert on your account (Equifax at 800-525-6285, Experian at 888-397-3742, and TransUnion at 800-680-7289). Also notify your banks including your credit card issuers, plus any creditors with whom the thief may have opened fraudulent accounts. File a report with the local police or sheriff's office, and inform the post office if you believe the thief has filed a change of address on your account.

2. Call the Federal Trade Commission's Identity Theft Hotline toll-free at (871) 438-4338.

3. Look up the Privacy Rights Clearinghouse, a non-profit consumer advocate program that has an excellent, helpful Web site at www.prc@privacyrights.org

ID theft is skyrocketing, aided by the fact that nearly 80 million American households have at least one credit card on which they charge a total of more than $1 trillion a year. Little wonder that this year about 600,000 consumers will have their identities stolen in one way or another, with 1 in 10 being victimized by credit card fraud. Unfortunately, when the victim runs to law enforcement agencies for assistance, any help they get will probably be very slow in coming. So will new federal laws to protect the average Joe and Jane cardholder.

To protect yourself, follow these tips:

- When you pay by credit card, cross out all the card numbers but the last four on your signed receipt. Draw lines through any empty spaces on that copy. Ask the merchant how it disposes of transaction slips and say good-bye if it doesn't sound safe.

- Reduce your credit cards to only one or two. Cancel any unused cards and, in writing, instruct the major credit bureaus that you don't want your credit records sold to "information brokers."

- Keep photocopies of your credit cards, including account numbers, expiration dates and customer service phone numbers in a secure place (not your wallet or purse) so you can quickly notify creditors if a card is stolen. Do the same thing for your bank account(s).

- Never give out your card numbers over the phone unless you have a trusted relationship with the company and you initiated the call.

- Order your credit report once a year from all three credit bureaus and study it for inaccuracies and fraudulent use of your accounts. Review monthly card statements carefully.

- Always' take your credit card receipts with you, and never toss them into public trash containers. Shred the receipts when they're no longer useful.

Keeping Score On Your Credit

If you've ever wondered what your credit rating is, now is your chance.

For the first time, consumers are being allowed to see their actual credit score, a number between 300 and 850 (the best rating) that tells lenders how good a credit risk you are.

This puts everyone on the same playing field, because consumers can now be aware of the information about them that creditors are privy to.

Until recently all you could see was your credit report, which listed any late payments or other financial problems that you had over the years. The actual number never was disclosed, except to lenders, because credit-rating agencies felt consumers wouldn't know how to interpret it.

But a new California disclosure law has prompted some of them to change that policy. Consumers anywhere in the country can now get their score, as well as a detailed explanation of how it was calculated. All you need is access to the Internet and $12.95.

There are two Web sites where you can get the score. One, **www.equifax.com**, is run by Equifax, one of the three major credit-rating agencies. The other, **www.myfico.com**, is run by FICO, the outfit that actually calculates the score. It doesn't matter which site you visit. The process, and cost, is the same.

Besides the score, you'll find out how it was calculated, how it compares with other consumers (average score: 720) and tips on how to improve it.

You also can see the same credit report that was available before from the three credit-rating services. Perhaps most important, you can still correct mistakes.

This gives you a chance to validate that information that may be harming your credit profile.

Unquestioned Fees Can Cost You A Bundle

When you took out your new mortgage or refinanced, did you ask why the fee for your credit report on the settlement sheet was $55 or $60? And did you ask what type of appraisal was conducted to justify the $300 or $400 you were charged?

If you're like the majority of mortgage borrowers, you probably didn't ask any detailed questions about settlement costs like these. Given the blur of paperwork, you may not have paid attention to them.

From now on, you need to. That's because credit and mortgage industry experts warn that technological advances have sharply reduced the underlying costs of credit and appraisal services, but that consumers frequently are charged outdated, and inflated, fees on their settlement sheets.

Those inflated fees violate federal law, but rarely are flagged by regulators.

Mortgage credit industry officials know that it's "an open secret." They mark up credit reports to $50 or $60 or whatever. Nobody's going to challenge them. One major mortgage company, according to industry sources, even gave an award at a December's employee Christmas party to the loan officer who originated the largest number of $60 bills to customers for credit reports that actually cost the company just $15 or less. The differential was pure profit for the firm.

Dramatic changes

The cost of credit bureau information to lenders has plunged dramatically in the past six years, far more than most consumers realize. The cost of the predominant type of credit report now used by lenders, an electronic "infile", is about $2.50. An infile is a quick drawdown of all the relevant information about a consumer on file at one of the three giant credit repositories, Equifax, Experian or Trans Union.

A single-repository infile for a married couple might cost the lender just $5. A "triple-merged" infile for the couple sorting out everything on file at all three repositories might go for $15. The highest volume commercial users of credit information get their data even cheaper, 60 cents or less per infile.

Traditional credit checks

As recently as the mid-1990s, by contrast, credit report costs to mortgage companies often were $45 to $55, and involved hands-on fact checking by local credit bureau personnel. That traditional form of credit check was used for 90 percent to 100 percent of all mortgage applications.

But today, according to credit industry estimates, barely 15 percent of new mortgage applications require anything beyond a merged infile. Yet many consumers are being charged for the full, hands-on report.

The National Credit Reporting Association, a trade group representing the independent credit bureaus who provide credit information to lenders across the country, acknowledges that this practice is quite common. The settlement sheet will say $60 or $55, but the actual cost was $15.

Mark-up is illegal

That mark-up, absent any additional work by the lender, is illegal. The department of Housing and Urban Development (HUD) said so in December 1999 in a case involving Washington Mutual Bank. HUD told a federal court that where lenders charge consumers marked-up prices for credit reports or other services, without performing any additional services, they are in violation of the law.

Lawyers representing mortgage lenders say they are aware of the mark-up practices and strongly advise against them.

These mark-up practices are referred to as a 'naked upcharge.' The rule is supposed to be that, if it costs the mortgage lender a dollar, they should charge the borrower a dollar.

Top legal experts in the field, say lenders caught doing performing mark-up practices risk federal suits and potential class actions by groups of overcharged borrowers.

Appraisals, Too

Mortgage brokers, .say the next big settlement cost category for illegal mark-ups almost certainly is appraisals. Increasingly lenders are using lower cost alternatives to traditional, full appraisals. Online data sources now produce property value estimates in minutes at minimal costs. Appraisers themselves frequently complain that they charge $175 for their work, but when the home buyer or refinancer sees the settlement sheet, the charge is $350.

How can you find out whether you're being up-charged on fees like these? Lenders themselves will tell you: Ask.

Lenders suggest that consumers ask to see the actual bill for the credit report if they have doubts. After all, it's supposed to be there in the files for auditors anyway, so lenders shouldn't object.

Bottom line: Don't end up as one of the price-gouged victims of the guy at the Christmas party, paying $60 without a peep for something the law says should be priced at $15.

Items Needed For Loan Application

1. Copy of Sales Agreement-Fully executed with all signatures.

2. Last Two (2) Months Bank Statements (i.e. checking, savings, money market, certificates of deposit, and Credit Union)

3. Savings Bonds-List of bond numbers and total value

4. Stock Evidence

5. Debts-Account Numbers, monthly payments, balances, and addresses

6. Gift letter and copy of gift check.

7. Employment History-Last two (2) years (Names and addresses of employers-Resume style)

8. W-2 Forms for the last two years

9. Copy of current Pay stubs (must cover 30 day period)

10. Self Employed:
    Two year Federal Income Tax Forms with ALL Schedules
    Year-to-Date Profit and Loss Statement and balance sheet

11. Disability, Retirement, Social Security Income verification

12. Divorce Papers-Copy of Separation Agreement AND Divorce Decree

13. Bankruptcy and Schedule:
    Copy of Bankruptcy Discharge Papers
    List of Creditors
    Statement of Financial Affairs

14.   Leases or rental agreements on investment properties

15.   VA Loans:
        DD214 Separation Paper
        Certificate of Eligibility

16.   Evidence of Social Security Number (pay stub, SS card, drivers license)

VA Buyer Qualification Worksheet

1. Principal & Interest   _____
2. Hazard Insurance   +_____
3. Property Taxes   +_____
4. Maintenance   +_____
5. Heat & Utilities   +_____
6. TOTAL HOUSING EXPENSES   =_____
7. PITI   _____
8. PLUS Fixed Debt
    (including child support/alimony,
    and/or child care)   +_____
9. Line 7+Line 8   =_____
10. Line 9/C   _____%

(Line 10 SHOULD NOT EXCEED 41-45%)
45% Total Ratio MAY BE exceeded if adequate residual is present, generally
    20% per additional 1% of ratio)

A. Gross Monthly Income   _____
B. Additional Income   +_____
C. TOTAL TAXABLE INCOME   =_____
    LESS:
            Federal Taxes   -_____
            Social Sec   -_____
            City Taxes   -_____
D. NET INCOME
E. Non-Taxable Income   +_____
F. TOTAL INCOME   =_____
G. LESS Fixed Debt   -_____
H. TOTAL EFFECTIVE INCOME   =_____
I. LESS housing expenses (Line 6)   -_____
J. EQUALS Balance Available for Residual   =_____

K.   Residual Needed from TABLE BELOW   _____

FAMILY SIZE	UNDER $70 000	OVER $70,000
1	$367	$424
2	$616	$710
3	$742	$855
4	$835	$964
5	$867	$999

FHA Buyer Qualification Worksheet

MONTHLY GROSS INCOME

Borrower's Base Pay	$_____
Co-Borrower's Base Pay	$_____
Other Income	$_____
TOTAL. INCOME	$_____
PREVIOUS MONTHLY HOUSING	$_____
29% of TOTAL INCOME	$_____
41% of TOTAL INCOME	$_____

*In new construction cases, the ratios are 31% and 43% due to energy efficient building standards.

PROPOSED MONTHLY PAYMENT

Principal & Interest	$_____
Taxes	$_____
Hazard Insurance	$_____
Monthly MIP	$_____
Second Mortgage Payment	$_____

Other $_____

TOTAL FIRST MORTGAGE PAYMENT $_____

TOTAL OF OTHER MONTHLY PAYMENTS
EXTENDING BEYOND TEN MONTHS
(Include applicable Alimony/Child
Support Payments) $_____

TOTAL OF ALL MONTHLY PAYMENTS $_____

Conventional Buyer Qualification Worksheet

MONTHLY GROSS INCOME

Borrower's Base Pay $_____

Co-Borrower's Base Pay $_____

Other Income $_____

TOTAL. INCOME $_____

PREVIOUS MONTHLY HOUSING $_____

28% of TOTAL INCOME $_____

36% of TOTAL INCOME $_____

*the ratios are a guideline and not to be construed as absolute. In many instances the borrower can exceed these ratios and in some cases the ratios would be too high. Ask your loan officer to pro-qualify the borrower.

PROPOSED MONTHLY PAYMENT

Principal & Interest $_____

Taxes $_____

Hazard Insurance $_____

Monthly MIP $_____

Second Mortgage Payment $_____

Other $_____

TOTAL FIRST AND SECOND
MORTGAGE PAYMENT $_____

TOTAL OF OTHER MONTHLY PAYMENTS
EXTENDING BEYOND TEN MONTHS
(Include applicable Alimony/Child
Support Payments) $_____

TOTAL OF ALL MONTHLY PAYMENTS $_____

Sample Appraisal

FRONT   REAR

SUBJECT PROPERTY

STREET SCENE   SHED

FOR SAMPLE APPRAISAL

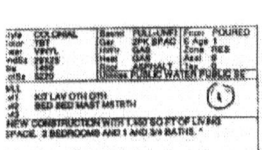 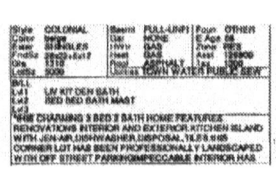 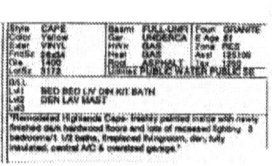

COMP 1   COMP 2   COMP 3

COMPARABLES FOR

Anywhere   STREET

FALL RIVER, MASSACHUSETTS

INCLUDING MLS DATA FOR THE 3 COMPARABLES.

UNIFORM RESIDENTIAL APPRAISAL REPORT File No.

Property Description

Property Address	City	State MA. Zip Code
Legal Description	County Bristol
Assessor's Parcel No.	Tax Year 02 R.E. Taxes $ Est 1500 Special Assessments $ 0
Borrower	Current Owner	Occupant [X] Owner [ ] Tenant [ ] Vacant
Property rights appraised [X] Fee Simple [ ] Leasehold Project Type [ ] PUD [ ] Condominium (HUD/VA only) HOA$ /Mo.
Neighborhood or Project Name None Known	Map Reference 7 A	Census Tract 6311
Sale Price $ n/a Date of Sale n/a Description and $ amount of loan charges/concessions to be paid by seller n/a
Lender/Client	Address
Appraiser John V. Medeiros	Address

Location	Urban	[X] Suburban	Rural	Predominant occupancy	Single family housing		Present land use %	Land use change
					PRICE $(000)	AGE (yrs)		
Built up	[X] Over 75%	26-75%	Under 25%				One family 100	[X] Not likely [ ] Likely
Growth rate	Rapid	[X] Stable	Slow	100 Owner %	130 Low 2		2-4 family	[ ] In process
Property values	Increasing	[X] Stable	Declining	Tenant	300 High 70		Multi-family	To:
Demand/supply	Shortage	[X] In balance	Over supply	[O] Vacant (0-5%)	Predominant		Commercial	
Marketing time	[X] Under 3 mos.	3-6 mos.	Over 6 mos.	Vacant (over 5%)	170	40		

Note: Race and the racial composition of the neighborhood are not appraisal factors.

Neighborhood boundaries and characteristics: THE SUBJECT PROPERTY IS BOUNDED BY: L_____ ___ ___ to the North, ___ to South, ___ st. to East, ___ Town Line co ___.

Factors that affect the marketability of the properties in the neighborhood (proximity to employment and amenities, employment stability, appeal to market, etc.): The Subject is conveniently located to Major and Local transportation, and to most amenities, and does have Market appeal,

SALES AND FINANCE CONCESSIONS ARE NOT PREVALENT AND DO NOT AFFECT SALES PRICES OF COMPARABLE HOMES. THE AVERAGE LISTING PRICE TO SALES PRICE RATIO IS 96 %

Market conditions in the subject neighborhood (including support for the above conclusions related to the trend of property values, demand/supply, and marketing time - - such as data on competitive properties for sale in the neighborhood, description of the prevalence of sales and financing concessions, etc.): I HAVE CONSIDERED RELEVANT COMPETITIVE LISTINGS AND/OR CONTRACT OFFERINGS IN THE PERFORMANCE OF THIS APPRAISAL AND IN THE TRENDING INFORMATION REPORTED IN THIS SECTION. IF ATREND IS INDICATED , I HAVE ATTACHED AN ADDENDUM PROVIDING RELEVANT COMPETITIVE LISTING/ CONTRACT OFFERING DATA. THE AVERAGE MARKETING TIME IN THIS NEIGHBORHOOD IS BETWEEN 60 TO 90 DAYS.

Project Information for PUDs (if applicable) - - Is the developer/builder in control of the Home Owners' Association (HOA)? [ ] Yes [ ] No
Approximate total number of units in the subject project ___ Approximate number of units for sale in the subject project ___
Describe common elements and recreational facilities: n/a

Site

Dimensions 80'X100'		Topography	Flat
Site area 8000 sq. ft.		Size	Typical
	Corner Lot [ ] Yes [X] No	Shape	Rectangular
Specific zoning classification and description Residential		Drainage	Seems adequate
Zoning compliance [X] Legal [ ] Legal nonconforming (Grandfathered use) [ ] Illegal [ ] No zoning		View	Average
Highest & best use as improved: [X] Present use [ ] Other use (explain)		Landscaping	Average

Utilities	Public	Other	Off-site improvements Type	Public	Private		
Electricity	[X]		Street Asphalt-Paved	[X]		Driveway Surface	Asphalt
Gas	[X]		Curb/gutter none			Apparent easements	none
Water	[X]		Sidewalk Grass		[X]	FEMA Special Flood Hazard Area [ ] Yes [X] No
Sanitary sewer	Indiv-Septi		Street lights		[X]	FEMA Zone C Map Date 5-29-81
Storm sewer			Alley none			FEMA Map No. 250049 0010 C

Comments (apparent adverse easements, encroachments, special assessments, slide areas, illegal or legal nonconforming zoning use, etc.): None Known or apparent.

Description of Improvements

GENERAL DESCRIPTION	EXTERIOR DESCRIPTION	FOUNDATION	BASEMENT	INSULATION
No. of Units 1	Foundation Concret	Slab	Area Sq. Ft. 825	Roof
No. of Stories 1.65	Exterior Walls Wood Shing.	Crawl Space	% Finished 0	Ceiling
Type (Det./Att.) Det.	Roof Surface Asph. Shing	Basement Full 100%	Ceiling Joist	Walls
Design (Style) Cottage	Gutters & Dwnspts. Alum.	Sump Pump None	Walls Cement	Floor
Existing/Proposed Exist.	Window Type Double Hung	Dampness none noted	Floor Cement	None
Age (Yrs.) 38	Storm/Screens Combos	Settlement none noted	Outside Entry Yes	Unknown [X]
Effective Age (Yrs.) 35	Manufactured House no	Infestation none noted		

ROOMS	Foyer	Living	Dining	Kitchen	Den	Family Rm.	Rec. Rm.	Bedrooms	# Baths	Laundry	Other	Area Sq. Ft.
Basement	/										F/Place	
Level 1		1	1	1				1	1.0			825
Level 2								2	.5			536

Finished area above grade contains: 6 Rooms; 3 Bedroom(s); 1.5 Bath(s); 1361 Square Feet of Gross Living Area

INTERIOR	Materials/Condition	HEATING		KITCHEN EQUIP.		ATTIC		AMENITIES		CAR STORAGE:	
Floors HD/Wd # Good		Type Hot Water		Refrigerator [X]		None		Fireplace(s) # L/R. [X]		None [X]	
Walls Drywall /Good		Fuel Gas		Range/Oven [X]		Stairs [X]		Patio		Garage # of cars	
Trim/Finish Good/Good		Condition Appear adequate		Disposal		Drop Stair		Deck	[X]	Attached	
Bath Floor Linoleum/G.		COOLING		Dishwasher		Scuttle		Porch	[X]	Detached	
Bath Wainscot Vinyl/Good		Central none		Fan/Hood [X]		Floor		Fence	[X]	Built-In	
Doors Wood, Flush/Good		Other none		Microwave [X]		Heated		Pool		Carport	
		Condition		Washer/Dryer [X]		Finished		Shed	[X]	Driveway 1 car	

Additional features (special energy efficient items, etc.): ___

Comments

Condition of the improvements, depreciation (physical, functional, and external), repairs needed, quality of construction, remodeling/additions, etc.: No repairs required. Subject has a Septic System and is subject to TITLE 5 Mass. regulations. Mrs. ___ claimed that anew system was installed when the house was purchased.

Adverse environmental conditions (such as, but not limited to, hazardous wastes, toxic substances, etc.) present in the improvements, on the site, or in the immediate vicinity of the subject property: None known or apparent

Freddie Mac Form 70 6-93 10 ch P37 Forms & Worms, Inc.   1(800) 243-4545 Item #112660 Fannie Mae Form 1004 6-93

UNIFORM RESIDENTIAL APPRAISAL REPORT   File No.

Valuation Section

COST APPROACH

ESTIMATED SITE VALUE .... = $ 50,000

ESTIMATED REPRODUCTION COST-NEW-OF IMPROVEMENTS:

Dwelling _____ Sq. Ft @ $ _____ = $ _____

_____ Sq. Ft @ $ _____ = _____   n/a

Garage/Carport _____ Sq. Ft @ $ _____ = _____

Total Estimated Cost New .... = $ _____

Less   Physical   Functional   External

Depreciation .... = $ _____

Depreciated Value of Improvements .... = $ _____

"As-is" Value of Site Improvements .... = $ _____

INDICATED VALUE BY COST APPROACH .... = $ _____ n/a

Comments on Cost Approach (such as, source of cost estimate site value, square foot calculation and for HUD, VA and FmHA, the estimated remaining economic life of the property): __40 yrs.__

GROSS LIVING AREA:
25'X33'=
825'x1.65 Sty.=
1361 sq. ft.

1.65 sq

33

25'

SALES COMPARISON ANALYSIS

ITEM	SUBJECT	COMPARABLE NO. 1		COMPARABLE NO. 2		COMPARABLE NO. 3	
Address							
Proximity to Subject		1/2 mile		7/8 mile		1/8 mile	
Sales Price	$ n/a		$ 150,000		$ 150,000		$ 60,000
Price/Gross Liv. Area	$ n/a ☒	$ n/a ☒		$ n/a ☒		$ n/a ☒	
Data and/or Verification Source	Public Records	MLS#		MLS#		MLS#	
VALUE ADJUSTMENTS	DESCRIPTION	DESCRIPTION	+ (-) $ Adjustment	DESCRIPTION	+ (-) $ Adjustment	DESCRIPTION	+ (-) $ Adjustment
Sales or Financing Concessions		Conventional Fin. none known	---	Conventional Fin. none known	---	Conventional Fin. none known	---
Date of Sale/Time		7-17-02	---	9-19-01	---	8-30-01	---
Location	Average	Average	---	Average	---	Average	---
Leasehold/Fee Simple	Fee	Fee	---	Fee	---	Fee	---
Site Sq. Ft.	8000	13,544	-2000	8605	---	10,000	-1000
View	Average	Average	---	Average	---	Average	---
Design and Appeal	Cottage	Cottage	---	Colonial	---	Cottage	---
Quality of Construction	Average	Average	---	Average	---	Average	---
Age YRS.	38	92	+5000	92	+5000	87	+5000
Condition	Good	Good	---	Good	---	Good	---
Above Grade Room Count	Total 6 / Bdrms 3 / Baths 1.5	Total 6 / Bdrms 3 / Baths 1.5	---	Total 7 / Bdrms 4 / Baths 1.0	±500	Total 6 / Bdrms 2 / Baths 1.0	+500
Gross Living Area	1491 Sq. Ft.	1496 Sq. Ft.	-2400	1698 Sq. Ft.	-6500	1200 Sq. Ft.	+3400
Basement & Finished Rooms Below Grade	100/0 %	100/0 %	---	100/0 %	---	100/0 %	---
Functional Utility	Good	Good	---	Good	---	Good	---
Heating/Cooling	Gas/none	Oil/none	---	Oil/none	---	Gas/Central	-300
Energy Efficient Items	Combos	Combos	---	Combos	---	Combos	---
Garage/Carport	None	1 Stall Det	-8000	none	---	none	---
Porch, Patio, Deck, etc.	Deck-Shed	---	+1000	Patio	+800	Enclosed porch	+800
Fireplace(s), etc.	1 F/Place	n0 f/place	+1500	1 F/Place	---	no f/place	+1500
Fence, Pool, etc.	Fence	---	+500	---	+500	---	+500
Net Adj. (total)		+ ☒ - $ 4400		☒ + - $ 300		☒ + - $ 9600	
Adjusted Sales Price of Comparable		$ 145,600		$ 150,300		$ 169,600	

Comments on Sales Comparison (including the subject property's compatibility to the neighborhood, etc.):

Time adjustment = none, Comp 1 is very recent. Comps 2 +3 are not too recent, but their locations are very close to the Subject, and the Market has been stable. Location adjustment = none, all Comps are within 1 mile of the Subject. Age adjustment=Subject is much younger than than all 3 Comps. Gross Living Area adjustment =$ 20 sq. ft.--More weight given to Comps 1 + 2.

ITEM	SUBJECT	COMPARABLE NO. 1	COMPARABLE NO. 2	COMPARABLE NO. 3
Date, Price and Data Source, for prior sales within year of appraisal	None Known	None Known	None Known	None Known

Analysis of any current agreement of sale, option, or listing of the subject property and analysis of any prior sales of subject and comparables within one year of the date of appraisal
None Known

RECONCILIATION

INDICATED VALUE BY SALES COMPARISON APPROACH .... $ 150,000

INDICATED VALUE BY INCOME APPROACH (If Applicable) Estimated Market Rent $ 1000 Mo. x Gross Rent Multiplier n/a = $ n/a

This appraisal is made ☒ "as is" ☐ subject to the repairs, alterations, inspections or conditions listed below ☐ subject to completion per plans and specifications.

Conditions of Appraisal: ____

Final Reconciliation: NOTE: THE COST AND INCOME APPROACHES TO VALUE ARE NOT HIGHLY RELIABLE SOURCES FOR THE ESTIMATION OF MARKET VALUE FOR SINGLE FAMILY RESIDENTIAL PROPERTIES, THEREFORE NOT UTILIZED.

The purpose of this appraisal is to estimate the market value of the real property that is the subject of this report ... the above conditions and the certification, contingent and limiting conditions, and market value definition that are stated in the attached Freddie Mac Form 439/Fannie M... ...40 (Revised ____).

I (WE) ESTIMATE THE MARKET VALUE, AS DEFINED, OF THE REAL PROPERTY THAT IS THE SUBJECT OF THIS REPORT, AS OF August 1, 2002 (WHICH IS THE DATE OF INSPECTION AND THE EFFECTIVE DATE OF THIS REPORT) TO BE $ 150,000

APPRAISER:	SUPERVISORY APPRAISER (ONLY IF REQUIRED):	
Signature	Signature	☐ Did ☐ Did Not
Name JOHN V. MEDEIROS	Name	Inspect Property
Date Report Signed August 1, 2002	Date Report Signed	
State Certification # 244	State Mass State Certification #	State
Or State License #	Or State License #	State

Freddie Mac Form 70 6-93   10 CH.   PAGE 2 OF 2   Fannie Mae Form 1004 6-1

SAMPLE APPRAISAL B

FRONT

REAR

SUBJECT PROPERTY

Somewhere STREET

R. I.

GARAGE

POOL

SINGLE FAMILY

List Price:$199,900 Area:
List Date: 05/16/02 **Sale Price:** $150,000
Exp Date: 09/16/02 **Sold Date:** 07/17/02
MLS#: **Status:** SLD
DOM: 4 **Off Mkt Date:** 05/20/02

Property Features

Rooms:	6	Style:	COLN
Bedrooms:	3	Type:	SF
Full Bath:	1	Acres:	0.31
Half Bath:	1	Lot Size:	13,544
Master Bath:	NO	GLA:	1496
Fireplace:	0	Fnd Size:	0
Year Blt:	1910	Color:	

Room Descriptions

Living Room:
Dining Room:
Family:
Kitchen:
Master BR:
Bedrm 2:
Bedrm 3:
Bedrm 4:
Bedrm 5:
Bath 1:
Bath 2:
Bath 3:
Laundry:
Other Room:

Feature	
Garage:	1 DETD
Waterfront:	NO
Basement:	YES
Exterior:	
Heat:	OIL
Cooling:	NONE
Hot Water:	
Electricity:	
Appliances:	
Interior:	
Exterior Feat:	
Construction:	
Roof:	ASFH
Road:	
Amenities:	
Sewer/Water:	CWTR, CSEW

Remarks: SPACIOUS 3 BR COLONIAL - OPEN FLOOR PLAN W/ HIGH CEILINGS
SHOWS BIGGER! NEW HEATING SYSTEM, FRESH PAINT, GREAT LOT
MOVE RIGHT IN, ENJOY THE PROTECTION OF AMERICAN HOME SHIELD
HOME WARRANTY, GOOD FOR 1 YEAR AFTER CLOSING!

Tax Information

Assessment:	$101,000
Taxes:	$1,596
Tax Year:	2001
Book/Page:	0/0
Certificate:	
Zoning:	RES
Map:	
Block:	
Lot:	

Listing Information

Directions:	READ YOUR MAP
Show Instr:	CALL OFC, CALL AGT. LKP'., DRCT
Office:	
Office Ph:	
Agent:	
Agent Ph:	
Sale Office:	
Sale Agent:	
Exclusions:	
Disclosures:	
Firm Remarks:	

Original List Price: $199,900
SAC: 2.5
OAC: BAC: 2.5

SINGLE FAMILY

List Price:$170,000 Area:
List Date: 07/14/01 Sale Price: $160,000
Exp Date: 11/14/01 Sold Date: 09/19/01
MLS#: Status: SLD
DOM: 19 Off Mkt Date:08/02/01

Property Features

Rooms:	7	Style:	COLN
Bedrooms:	4	Type:	SF
Full Bath:	1	Acres:	0.19
Half Bath:	0	Lot Size:	8,605
Master Bath:	NO	GLA:	1698
Fireplace:	1	Fnd Size:	30X28
Year Blt:	1910	Color:	TAN

Room Descriptions

Living Room:	1 FRPL, FANS, HDWD
Dining Room:	1 HDWD
Family:	
Kitchen:	1 HBTH
Master BR:	2 FANS, HDWD
Bedrm 2:	2 HDWD
Bedrm 3:	2 FANS, HDWD
Bedrm 4:	2 FANS, HDWD
Bedrm 5:	
Bath 1:	2
Bath 2:	
Bath 3:	
Laundry:	
Other Room:	

Features

Garage:	0
Waterfront:	NO
Basement:	YES
Exterior:	CLAP
Heat:	STEM, OIL
Cooling:	NONE
Hot Water:	ELEC, TANK
Electricity:	220V, CIRC, 100A
Appliances:	RNGE, REFG
Interior:	
Exterior Feat:	PATO, GUTT, STRG
Construction:	FRAM
Roof:	ASFH
Road:	PBLC, PUMN, DEAD
Amenities:	TRAN, GOLF, LDMT
Sewer/Water:	CWTR, PSEW

Remarks: FOUR BEDROOM COLONIAL AT END OF STREET. HOME HAS HARDWOOD FLOORS AND A FIREPLACE IN THE LIVING ROOM. PRIVATE PATIO ON BACKYARD.

Tax Information

Assessment:	$105,500
Taxes:	$1,866
Tax Year:	2001
Book/Page:	
Certificate:	
Zoning:	RES
Map:	
Block:	
Lot:	

Listing Information

Directions:	
Show Instr:	
Office:	
Office Ph:	
Agent:	
Agent Ph:	
Sale Office:	
Sale Agent:	
Exclusions:	
Disclosures:	2ND BATH IN BSMT NOT CONNECTED TO PUBLIC
Firm Remarks:	

Original List Price:
$170,000
SAC: 3
OAC: BAC: 3

Phone:

(Cont ③) ½ mile

SINGLE FAMILY

List Price: $162,000 Area:
List Date: 06/26/01 Sale Price: $160,000
Exp Date: 10/26/01 Sold Date: 08/30/01
MLS#: Status: SLD
DOM: 50 Off Mkt Date: 08/15/01

Property Features

Rooms:	6	Style:	CAPE
Bedrooms:	2	Type:	SF
Full Bath:	1	Acres:	0.23
Half Bath:	0	Lot Size:	10,000
Master Bath:	NO	GLA:	1200
Fireplace:	0	Fnd Size:	26X40
Year Blt:	1915	Color:	

Room Descriptions

Living Room:	1	Garage:	0
Dining Room:	1	Waterfront:	NO
Family:		Basement:	YES
Kitchen:	1	Exterior:	VNYL
Master BR:	1	Heat:	FRAR, GAS
Bedrm 2:	1	Cooling:	CAIR
Bedrm 3:		Hot Water:	NGAS, TANK
Bedrm 4:		Electricity:	CIRC, 100A
Bedrm 5:		Appliances:	RNGE, REFG
Bath 1:	1	Interior:	
Bath 2:		Exterior Feat:	EPCH
Bath 3:		Construction:	FRAM
Laundry:		Roof:	ASFH
Other Room:		Road:	PBLC
		Amenities:	TRAN, SHOP
		Sewer/Water:	CWTR, CSEW

Features

Remarks: EXCEPTIONAL OPPORTUNITY!NICE OPEN FLOOR PLAN WITH 2 BDRMS
WITH WALK-UP ATTIC AND PLENTY OF ROOM TO EXPAND* CENTRAL
AIR* ENCLOSED FRONT PORCH*CITY WATER & SEWER*UPDATING NEEDED

Tax Information

Assessment:	$108,300
Taxes:	$1,661
Tax Year:	2001
Book/Page:	
Certificate:	
Zoning:	SFR
Map:	
Block:	
Lot:	

Listing Information

Directions:
Show Instr:
Office:
Office Ph:
Agent:
Agent Ph:
Sale Office:
Sale Agent:
Exclusions:
Disclosures: RENTED BURNER BUN ON FURNACE
Firm Remarks:

Original List Price: $162,000
SAC: 3.0
BAC: 3.0
OAC:
Phone:
Phone:

SAMPLE APPRAISAL

UNIFORM RESIDENTIAL APPRAISAL REPORT File No.

Property Address: Somewhere Street City State R.I. Zip Code 02920

Legal Description: Book -Page County Providence Cou

Assessor's Parcel No. Plat -Lot Tax Year 01 RE Taxes $ 7216 Special Assessments $ 0

Property rights appraised [X] Fee Simple [ ] Leasehold Project Type [ ] PUD [ ] Condominium (HUD/VA only) HOA$

Neighborhood or Project Name None Known Map Reference Census Tract

Sale Price $ 157,000 Date of Sale 7-05-01 None Known

Lender/Client Home Mtg. Address

Appraiser John V. Medeiros Address 89 Norwood St. Seekonk, Mass. 02777

THE SUBJECT PROPERTY IS BOUNDED BY: ATWOOD AVE. THE EA
PHOENIX AVE. TO THE WEST; CRANSTON ST. TO THE SOUTH; AND ENTERPRISE ST. TO N

THE SUBJECT IS CONVENIENT TO LOCAL AND MAJOR TRANSPORTATION, AND TO MOST
AMENITIES, AND DOES HAVE MARKET APPEAL.
SALES AND FINANCE CONCESSIONS ARE NOT PREVALENT AND DO NOT AFFECT SALES
PRICES OF COMPARABLE HOMES.
THE AVERAGE LISTING PRICE TO SALES PRICE RATIO IS 98 %

I HAVE CONSIDERED RELEVANT COMPETITIVE LISTINGS AND/OR CONTRACT OFFENING
IN THE PERFORMANCE OF THIS APPRAISAL AND IN THE TRENDING INFORMATION REPORT
IN THIS SECTION. IF A TREND IS INDICATED I HAVE ATTACHED AN ADDENDUM PROVI
RELEVANT COMPETITIVE LISTING/ CONTRACT OFFERING DATA. THE AVERAGE MARKETIN
TIME IN THIS NEIGHBORHOOD IS SIX WEEKS.

Dimensions 70 x 80
Site area 5600 sq. ft.
Zoning classification residential

Topography Flat
typical
Size Squareish
Shape Seems adequate
Drainage Average
View Average
Landscaping Average
Driveway Surface Asphalt-paved
Apparent easements none
FEMA Zone I=1=1
FEMA Map No. 445396-0005 B

Off-site improvements Street Asphalt-Paved
Alley None

Comments: None known or apparent

GENERAL DESCRIPTION
No. of Units 1
No. of Stories 1.0
Type (Det./Att.) Det.
Design (Style) Ranch
Existing/Proposed Exist.
Age (Yrs.) 50
Effective Age (Yrs.) 35

EXTERIOR DESCRIPTION
Foundation Concrete
Exterior Walls Vinyl
Roof Surface Asph Shin.
Gutters & Dwnspts. Alum.
Window Type Double Hung
Storm/Screens Combos/yes
Manufactured House No

FOUNDATION
Slab ---
Crawl Space ---
Basement Full
Sump Pump No
Dampness none noted
Settlement none noted
Infestation none noted

BASEMENT
Area Sq. Ft. 972
% Finished 95
Ceiling Panel
Walls Panel
Floor Lin. #cement
Outside Entry No

ROOMS: Level 1 — Living 1, Kitchen 1, Den 1, Bedrooms 3, # Baths 1.5 — Area 135

Finished area above grade contains: Rooms 3 Bedrooms 1.5 Baths 1355 Square Feet of Gross Liv

INTERIOR Materials/Condition
Floors Hd/wd /good
Walls Panel / good
Trim/Finish Good/Good
Bath Floor Tile /Good
Bath Wainscot Tile/ Good
Doors Wood/flush/Good

HEATING Hot
Type Water
Fuel Oil

COOLING none
Central none
Other none

KITCHEN EQUIP.
Refrigerator
Range/Oven
Disposal
Dishwasher
Fan/Hood
Microwave
Washer/Dryer

ATTIC
None
Stairs
Drop Stair
Scuttle
Floor
Heated
Finished

AMENITIES
Fireplace(s)
Patio
Deck
Porch
Fence In-Ground
Pool Dreway

CAR STORAGE
None
Garage
Attached X
Detached
Built-In
Carport
Driveway

Additional features: 3 Overhead Fans in bedrooms.

Condition of the improvements: No repairs required. The subject is in very good condition--both Inter
and Exterior.

Adverse environmental conditions: None known or apparent

SAMPLE APPRAISAL

UNIFORM RESIDENTIAL APPRAISAL REPORT   File No.

ESTIMATED SITE VALUE . . . . = $ 50,000

NOTE: THE COST AND INCOME APPROACHES TO VALUE ARE NOT HIGHLY RELIABLE SOURCES FOR THE ESTIMATION OF MARKET VALUE FOR SINGLE FAMILY RESIDENTIAL PROPERTIES, THEREFORE NOT UTILIZED.

Name: JOHN V. MEDEIROS

Date Report Signed: JULY 26, 2001

State Certification #: 244

Mortgage Loan Payment Factors Per $1000

INTEREST RATE	30-YEAR LOAN	20-YEAR LOAN	15-YEAR LOAN
10.000%	$8.775716	$9.650216	$10.746051
9.875%	$8.683486	$9.567545	$10.669709
9.750%	$8.591544	$9.485169	$10.593627
9.625%	$8.499894	$9.403090	$10.517805
9.500%	$8.408542	$9.321312	$10.442247
9.375%	$8.317494	$9.239837	$10.366952
9.250%	$8.226754	$9.158668	$10.291923
9.125%	$8.136330	$9.077808	$10.217160
9.000%	$8.046226	$8.997260	$10.142666
8.875%	$7.956449	$8.917025	$10.068441
8.750%	$7.867004	$8.837107	$9.994487
8.625%	$7.777897	$8.757509	$9.920804
8.500%	$7.689135	$8.678232	$9.847396
8.375%	$7.600722	$8.599281	$9.774262
8.250%	$7.512666	$8.520657	$9.701404
8.125%	$7.424972	$8.442362	$9.628823
8.000%	$7.337646	$8.364401	$9.556521
7.875%	$7.250694	$8.286774	$9.484499
7.750%	$7.164122	$8.209486	$9.412758
7.625%	$7.077937	$8.132537	$9.341299
7.500%	$6.992145	$8.055932	$9.270124
7.375%	$6.906751	$7.979672	$9.199233
7.250%	$6.821763	$7.903760	$9.128629
7.125%	$6.737185	$7.828198	$9.058312
7.000%	$6.653025	$7.752989	$8.988283
6.875%	$6.569288	$7.678136	$8.918543
6.750%	$6.485981	$7.603640	$8.849095
6.625%	$6.403110	$7.529504	$8.779938
6.500%	$6.320680	$7.455731	$8.711074
6.375%	$6.238699	$7.382323	$8.642504
6.250%	$6.157172	$7.309282	$8.574229

6.125%	$6.076105	$7.236610	$8.506250
6.000%	$5.995505	$7.164311	$8.438568
5.875%	$5.915378	$7.092385	$8.371185
5.750%	$5.835729	$7.020835	$8.304101
5.625%	$5.756564	$6.949664	$8.237317
5.500%	$5.677890	$6.878873	$8.170835
5.375%	$5.599712	$6.808465	$8.104654
5.250%	$5.522037	$6.738442	$8.038777
5.125%	$5.444870	$6.668805	$7.973204
5.000%	$5.368216	$6.599557	$7.907936

Conventional Loan Payment Factors For Monthly Payments Per $1,000

Conventional Loan Payment Factors For Monthly Payments Per $1,000

Rate Years	6	6.25	6.5	6.75	7	7.25	7.5	7.75	8
1	86.0664	86.1814	86.2964	86.4115	86.5267	86.6420	86.7574	86.8729	86.9884
2	44.3206	44.4333	44.5463	44.6593	44.7726	44.8860	44.9996	45.1134	45.2273
3	30.4219	30.5353	30.6490	30.7629	30.8771	30.9915	31.1062	31.2212	31.3364
4	23.4850	23.5998	23.7150	23.8304	23.9462	24.0624	24.1789	24.2957	24.4129
5	19.3328	19.4493	19.5661	19.6835	19.8012	19.9194	20.0379	20.1570	20.2764
6	16.5729	16.6912	16.8099	16.9292	17.0490	17.1693	17.2901	17.4114	17.5332
7	14.6086	14.7287	14.8494	14.9708	15.0927	15.2152	15.3383	15.4620	15.5862
8	13.1414	13.2635	13.3862	13.5096	13.6337	13.7585	13.8839	14.0099	14.1367
9	12.0057	12.1298	12.2545	12.3800	12.5063	12.6333	12.7610	12.8895	13.0187
10	11.1021	11.2280	11.3548	11.4824	11.6108	11.7401	11.8702	12.0011	12.1328
11	10.3670	10.4949	10.6238	10.7535	10.8841	11.0156	11.1480	11.2813	11.4154
12	9.7585	9.8884	10.0192	10.1510	10.2838	10.4176	10.5523	10.6879	10.8245
13	9.2472	9.3790	9.5119	9.6458	9.7807	9.9167	10.0537	10.1917	10.3307
14	8.8124	8.9461	9.0810	9.2169	9.3540	9.4922	9.6314	9.7718	9.9132
15	8.4386	8.5742	8.7111	8.8491	8.9883	9.1286	9.2701	9.4128	9.5565
16	8.1144	8.2519	8.3908	8.5308	8.6721	8.8146	8.9583	9.1032	9.2493
17	7.8310	7.9705	8.1112	8.2533	8.3966	8.5412	8.6871	8.8342	8.9826
18	7.5816	7.7229	7.8656	8.0096	8.1550	8.3017	8.4497	8.5990	8.7496
19	7.3608	7.5040	7.6486	7.7945	7.9419	8.0907	8.2408	8.3922	8.5450
20	7.1643	7.3093	7.4557	7.6036	7.7530	7.9038	8.0559	8.2095	8.3644
21	6.9886	7.1353	7.2836	7.4334	7.5847	7.7375	7.8917	8.0473	8.2043
22	6.8307	6.9793	7.1294	7.2811	7.4342	7.5889	7.7451	7.9027	8.0618
23	6.6885	6.8387	6.9906	7.1441	7.2992	7.4558	7.6139	7.7735	7.9345
24	6.5598	6.7118	6.8654	7.0207	7.1776	7.3361	7.4960	7.6576	7.8205
25	6.4430	6.5967	6.7521	6.9091	7.0678	7.2281	7.3899	7.5533	7.7182
26	6.3368	6.4921	6.6492	6.8079	6.9684	7.1304	7.2941	7.4593	7.6260
27	6.2399	6.3968	6.5555	6.7160	6.8781	7.0419	7.2073	7.3743	7.5428
28	6.1512	6.3098	6.4702	6.6323	6.7961	6.9616	7.1287	7.2974	7.4676

29	6.0700	6.2302	6.3921	6.5558	6.7213	6.8884	7.0572	7.2276	7.3995
30	5.9955	6.1572	6.3207	6.4860	6.6530	6.8218	6.9921	7.1641	7.3376
31	5.9269	6.0901	6.2552	6.4220	6.5906	6.7609	6.9328	7.1064	7.2815
32	5.8638	6.0284	6.1950	6.3633	6.5334	6.7052	6.8787	7.0538	7.2304
33	5.8055	5.9716	6.1396	6.3094	6.4810	6.6543	6.8292	7.0057	7.1838
34	5.7517	5.9192	6.0886	6.2598	6.4328	6.6075	6.7839	6.9619	7.1414
35	5.7019	5.8708	6.0415	6.2142	6.3886	6.5647	6.7424	6.9218	7.1026
36	5.6558	5.8260	5.9981	6.1721	6.3478	6.5253	6.7044	6.8850	7.0672
37	5.6130	5.7845	5.9580	6.1333	6.3103	6.4891	6.6694	6.8514	7.0348
38	5.5733	5.7461	5.9208	6.0974	6.2757	6.4557	6.6374	6.8205	7.0052
39	5.5364	5.7105	5.8864	6.0642	6.2438	6.4250	6.6079	6.7922	6.9780
40	5.5021	5.6774	5.8546	6.0336	6.2143	6.3967	6.5807	6.7662	6.9531

Conventional Loan Payment Factors For Monthly Payments Per $1,000

Years	Rate 8.25	8.5	8.75	9	9.25	9.5	9.75	10	10.25
1	87.1041	87.2198	87.3356	87.4515	87.5675	87.6835	87.7997	87.9159	88.0322
2	45.3414	45.4557	45.5701	45.6847	45.7995	45.9145	46.0296	46.1449	46.2604
3	31.4518	31.5675	31.6835	31.7997	31.9162	32.0329	32.1499	32.2672	32.3847
4	24.5304	24.6483	24.7665	24.8850	25.0039	25.1231	25.2427	25.3626	25.4828
5	20.3963	20.5165	20.6372	20.7584	20.8799	21.0019	21.1242	21.2470	21.3703
6	17.6556	17.7784	17.9017	18.0255	18.1499	18.2747	18.4000	18.5258	18.6522
7	15.7111	15.8365	15.9625	16.0891	16.2162	16.3440	16.4723	16.6012	16.7306
8	14.2641	14.3921	14.5208	14.6502	14.7802	14.9109	15.0422	15.1742	15.3068
9	13.1487	13.2794	13.4108	13.5429	13.6758	13.8094	13.9437	14.0787	14.2144
10	12.2653	12.3986	12.5327	12.6676	12.8033	12.9398	13.0770	13.2151	13.3539
11	11.5505	11.6864	11.8232	11.9608	12.0993	12.2386	12.3788	12.5199	12.6618
12	10.9621	11.1006	11.2400	11.3803	11.5216	11.6637	11.8068	11.9508	12.0957
13	10.4708	10.6118	10.7538	10.8968	11.0408	11.1857	11.3316	11.4785	11.6263
14	10.0557	10.1992	10.3438	10.4894	10.6360	10.7837	10.9324	11.0820	11.2327
15	9.7014	9.8474	9.9945	10.1427	10.2919	10.4422	10.5936	10.7461	10.8995
16	9.3965	9.5449	9.6945	9.8452	9.9970	10.1499	10.3039	10.4590	10.6152
17	9.1321	9.2829	9.4349	9.5880	9.7423	9.8978	10.0544	10.2121	10.3709
18	8.9015	9.0546	9.2089	9.3644	9.5212	9.6791	9.8382	9.9984	10.1598
19	8.6991	8.8545	9.0111	9.1690	9.3281	9.4884	9.6499	9.8126	9.9764
20	8.5207	8.6782	8.8371	8.9973	9.1587	9.3213	9.4852	9.6502	9.8164
21	8.3627	8.5224	8.6834	8.8458	9.0094	9.1743	9.3405	9.5078	9.6763
22	8.2222	8.3841	8.5472	8.7117	8.8775	9.0446	9.2129	9.3825	9.5532
23	8.0970	8.2609	8.4261	8.5927	8.7606	8.9297	9.1002	9.2718	9.4447
24	7.9850	8.1508	8.3181	8.4866	8.6566	8.8277	9.0002	9.1739	9.3488
25	7.8845	8.0523	8.2214	8.3920	8.5638	8.7370	8.9114	9.0870	9.2638
26	7.7942	7.9638	8.1348	8.3072	8.4810	8.6560	8.8323	9.0098	9.1885
27	7.7128	7.8842	8.0570	8.2313	8.4068	8.5836	8.7617	8.9410	9.1214
28	7.6393	7.8125	7.9871	8.1630	8.3403	8.5188	8.6986	8.8796	9.0618
29	7.5729	7.7477	7.9240	8.1016	8.2805	8.4607	8.6421	8.8248	9.0085
30	7.5127	7.6891	7.8670	8.0462	8.2268	8.4085	8.5915	8.7757	8.9610
31	7.4581	7.6361	7.8155	7.9963	8.1783	8.3616	8.5461	8.7318	8.9185
32	7.4085	7.5880	7.7689	7.9512	8.1347	8.3194	8.5053	8.6924	8.8805
33	7.3634	7.5444	7.7267	7.9103	8.0953	8.2814	8.4687	8.6570	8.8465
34	7.3223	7.5047	7.6884	7.8734	8.0596	8.2471	8.4356	8.6253	8.8159
35	7.2849	7.4686	7.6536	7.8399	8.0274	8.2161	8.4059	8.5967	8.7886
36	7.2508	7.4358	7.6220	7.8096	7.9983	8.1882	8.3791	8.5710	8.7640
37	7.2196	7.4058	7.5933	7.7820	7.9719	8.1629	8.3549	8.5479	8.7419
38	7.1912	7.3786	7.5672	7.7570	7.9480	8.1400	8.3331	8.5271	8.7221
39	7.1652	7.3537	7.5434	7.7343	7.9263	8.1193	8.3134	8.5084	8.7042
40	7.1414	7.3309	7.5217	7.7136	7.9066	8.1006	8.2956	8.4915	8.6882

Conventional Loan Payment Factors For Monthly Payments Per $1,000

Rate Years	10.5	10.75	11	11.25	11.5	11.75	12	12.25	12.5
1	88.1486	88.2651	88.3817	88.4983	88.6151	88.7319	88.8488	88.9658	89.0829
2	46.3760	46.4919	46.6078	46.7240	46.8403	46.9568	47.0735	47.1903	47.3073
3	32.5024	32.6205	32.7387	32.8572	32.9760	33.0950	33.2143	33.3338	33.4536
4	25.6034	25.7243	25.8455	25.9671	26.0890	26.2113	26.3338	26.4568	26.5800
5	21.4939	21.6180	21.7424	21.8673	21.9926	22.1183	22.2444	22.3710	22.4979
6	18.7790	18.9063	19.0341	19.1624	19.2912	19.4204	19.5502	19.6804	19.8112
7	16.8607	16.9913	17.1224	17.2542	17.3865	17.5193	17.6527	17.7867	17.9212
8	15.4400	15.5739	15.7084	15.8436	15.9794	16.1158	16.2528	16.3905	16.5288
9	14.3509	14.4880	14.6259	14.7644	14.9037	15.0436	15.1842	15.3256	15.4676
10	13.4935	13.6339	13.7750	13.9169	14.0595	14.2029	14.3471	14.4920	14.6376
11	12.8045	12.9480	13.0923	13.2375	13.3835	13.5303	13.6779	13.8263	13.9754
12	12.2414	12.3880	12.5356	12.6839	12.8332	12.9833	13.1342	13.2860	13.4386
13	11.7750	11.9247	12.0753	12.2268	12.3792	12.5325	12.6867	12.8417	12.9977
14	11.3843	11.5370	11.6905	11.8451	12.0006	12.1570	12.3143	12.4725	12.6317
15	11.0540	11.2095	11.3660	11.5234	11.6819	11.8413	12.0017	12.1630	12.3252
16	10.7724	10.9307	11.0900	11.2503	11.4116	11.5740	11.7373	11.9015	12.0667
17	10.5308	10.6918	10.8538	11.0169	11.1810	11.3461	11.5122	11.6792	11.8473
18	10.3223	10.4858	10.6505	10.8162	10.9830	11.1507	11.3195	11.4893	11.6600
19	10.1414	10.3075	10.4746	10.6429	10.8122	10.9825	11.1539	11.3262	11.4995
20	9.9838	10.1523	10.3219	10.4926	10.6643	10.8371	11.0109	11.1856	11.3614
21	9.8460	10.0168	10.1887	10.3617	10.5358	10.7109	10.8870	11.0641	11.2422
22	9.7251	9.8981	10.0722	10.2475	10.4237	10.6011	10.7794	10.9587	11.1390
23	9.6187	9.7938	9.9701	10.1474	10.3258	10.5052	10.6856	10.8670	11.0494
24	9.5248	9.7020	9.8803	10.0596	10.2400	10.4214	10.6038	10.7872	10.9714
25	9.4418	9.6209	9.8011	9.9824	10.1647	10.3480	10.5322	10.7174	10.9035
26	9.3683	9.5492	9.7313	9.9143	10.0984	10.2835	10.4695	10.6565	10.8443
27	9.3030	9.4857	9.6695	9.8543	10.0401	10.2268	10.4145	10.6030	10.7925
28	9.2450	9.4294	9.6148	9.8012	9.9886	10.1769	10.3661	10.5562	10.7471
29	9.1934	9.3793	9.5663	9.7542	9.9431	10.1329	10.3236	10.5151	10.7074
30	9.1474	9.3348	9.5232	9.7126	9.9029	10.0941	10.2861	10.4790	10.6726
31	9.1063	9.2952	9.4850	9.6757	9.8673	10.0598	10.2531	10.4472	10.6420
32	9.0697	9.2598	9.4509	9.6429	9.8358	10.0295	10.2240	10.4192	10.6152
33	9.0369	9.2283	9.4206	9.6138	9.8079	10.0027	10.1983	10.3946	10.5916
34	9.0076	9.2002	9.3936	9.5880	9.7831	9.9790	10.1756	10.3729	10.5708
35	8.9813	9.1750	9.3696	9.5649	9.7611	9.9579	10.1555	10.3537	10.5525
36	8.9578	9.1526	9.3481	9.5445	9.7415	9.9393	10.1378	10.3368	10.5365
37	8.9368	9.1325	9.3290	9.5262	9.7242	9.9228	10.1221	10.3219	10.5223
38	8.9179	9.1145	9.3119	9.5100	9.7087	9.9082	10.1082	10.3088	10.5099
39	8.9009	9.0984	9.2966	9.4955	9.6950	9.8952	10.0959	10.2971	10.4989
40	8.8857	9.0840	9.2829	9.4826	9.6828	9.8836	10.0850	10.2869	10.4892

Monthly Payment To Principal And Interest Rate Per $1,000

Interest Rate	Maximum Term in Years	Maximum Term in Months	Number of Payments	Initial Curtail Rates	Monthly Payment to Principal and Interest Rate per $1,000*
6 ¾ %	40	0	480	0.490282 %	$6.033568
6 ¾	35	0	420	0.706998	6.214165
6 ¾	30	0	360	1.033177	6.485981
6 ¾	25	0	300	1.540938	6.909115
6 ¾	20	0	240	2.374368	7.603640
6 ¾	15	0	180	3.868914	8.849095
6 ¾	10	0	120	7.028893	11.482411
6 ½	40	0	480	0.525482	5.854568
6 ½	35	0	420	0.749852	6.041543
6 ½	30	0	360	1.084816	6.320680
6 ½	25	0	300	1.602486	6.752072
6 ½	20	0	240	2.446877	7.455731
6 ½	15	0	180	3.953289	8.711074
6 ½	10	0	120	7.125758	11.354798
6 ¼	40	0	480	0.562875	5.677396
6 ¼	35	0	420	0.794918	5. 870765
6 ¼	30	0	360	1.138606	6.157172
6 ¼	25	0	300	1.666033	6.596694
6 ¼	20	0	240	2.521138	7.309282
6 ¼	15	0	180	4.039075	8.574229
6 ¼	10	0	120	7.223612	11.228010
6	40	0	480	0.602563	5. 502136
6	35	0	420	0.842276	5.701897
6	30	0	360	1.194606	5.995505
6	25	0	300	1.731617	6. 443014
6	20	0	240	2.597173	7.164311
6	15	0	180	4.126282	8.438568
6	10	0	120	7.322460	11.102050

Interest Rate	Maximum Term in Years	Maximum Term in Months	Number of Payments	Initial Curtail Rates	Monthly Payment to Principal and Interest Rate per $1,000*
5 ¾	40	0	480	0.644651	5.328876
5 ¾	35	0	420	0.892008	5.535007
5 ¾	30	0	360	1.252875	5. 835729
5 ¾	25	0	300	1.799277	6.291064
5 ¾	20	0	240	2.675002	7.020835
5 ¾	15	0	180	4.214921	8.304101
5 ¾	10	0	120	7.422306	10.976922
5 ½	40	0	480	0.689244	5.157703
5 ½	35	0	420	0.944196	5.370163
5 ½	30	0	360	1.313468	5.677890
5 ½	25	0	300	1.869050	6.140875
5 ½	20	0	240	2.754648	6.878873
5 ½	15	0	180	4. 305002	8.170835
5 ½	10	0	120	7. 523154	10.852628
5 ¼	40	0	480	0.736444	4.988703
5 ¼	35	0	420	0.998916	5.207430
5 ¼	30	0	360	1.376444	5.522037
5 ¼	25	0	300	1.940972	5.992477
5 ¼	20	0	240	2.836130	6.738442
5 ¼	15	0	180	4.396532	8.038777
5 ¼	10	0	120	7 .625004	10.729170
3	40	0	480	1.295813	3.579844
3	35	0	420	1. 618202	3.848502
3	30	0	360	2.059248	4.216040
3	25	0	300	2.690536	4.742113
3	20	0	240	3.655171	5.545976
3	15	0	180	5.286979	6.905816
3	10	0	120	8. 587289	9.656074
2	40	0	480	1.633907	3.028256
2	35	0	420	1.975154	3.312628
2	30	0	360	2.435434	3.696195
2	25	0	300	3.086252	4.238543
2	20	0	240	4.070600	5.058833
2	15	0	180	5.722104	6.435087
2	10	0	120	9.04163.4	9.201345
1	40	0	480	2.034273	2.528561
1	35	0	420	2.387428	2.822857
1	30	0	360	2.859675	3.216396
1	25	0	300	3.522471	3.768726
1	20	0	240	4.518733	4.598944
1	15	0	180	6.181935	5.984946
1	10	0	120	9. 512496	8.760413

*The monthly payment for a loan on the Level Annuity Monthly Payment basis is calculated by dividing the mortgage amount by 1,000, multiplying the result by the applied figure in the Monthly Payment. to Principal column and rounding to the next higher whole cent.

Monthly Payment To Principal And Interest Per $1,000 For A 40 Year Term

Interest Rate %	Initial Curtail %	Service Charge or MIP	Debt Service Rate %	Override Return on Investment	Cap Rate %	Net Income Multiplier	Monthly Payment to Principal and Interest per Thousand
7.5	0.396850	0.5 %	8.396850	0.5 %	8.896850	11.24	$6.580708
8.0	0.343740	0.5	8.843740	0.5	9.334740	10.71	6.953117
8.5	0.297129	0.5	9.297129	0.5	9.797129	10.21	7.330941
9.0	0.256338	0.5	9.756338	0.5	10.256338	9.75	7.713615
9.5	0.220739	0.5	10.220739	0.5	10.720739	9.33	8.100616
10.0	0.189751	0.5	10.689751	0.5	11.189751	8.94	8.491459
10.5	0.162844	0.5	11.162844	0.5	11.662844	8.57	8.885703
11.0	0.139533	0.5	11.639533	0.5	12.139533	8.24	9.282944
11.5	0.119383	0.5	12.119383	0.5	12.619383	7.92	9.682819
12.0	0.102000	0.5	12.602000	0.5	13.102000	7.63	10.085000
12.5	0.087033	0.5	13.087033	0.25	13.337033	7.50	10.489194
13.0	0.074170	0.5	13.574170	0.25	13.824170	7.23	10.895142
13.5	0.063135	0.5	14.063135	0.25	14.313135	6.99	11.302613
14.0	0.053681	0.5	14.553681	0.25	14.803681	6.76	11.711401
14.5	0.045596	0.5	15.045596	0.25	15.295596	6.54	12.121330
15.0	0.038690	0.5	15.538690	0.25	15.788690	6.33	12.532242
15.5	0.032800	0.5	16.032800	0.25	16.282800	6.14	12.944000
16.0	0.027782	0.5	16.527782	0.25	16.717782	5.96	13.356485

Glossary

203(b): FHA program which provides mortgage insurance to protect lenders from default; used to finance the purchase of new or existing one-to four-family housing; characterized by low down payment, flexible qualifying guidelines, limited fees, and a limit on maximum loan amount

203(k): this FHA mortgage insurance program enables homebuyers to finance both the purchase of a house and the cost of its rehabilitation through a single mortgage loan

A

Amenity: a feature of the home or property that serves as a benefit to the buyer but that is not necessary to its use; may be natural (like location, woods, water) or man-made (like a swimming pool or garden)

Amortization: repayment of a mortgage loan through monthly installments of principal and interest; the monthly payment amount is based on a schedule that will allow you to own your home at the end of a specific time period (for example, 15 or 30 years)

Anchor Bolt: A bolt usually 12 inches or longer which when imbedded in the foundation wall at intervals serves to anchor the building to the foundation.

Annual Percentage Rate (APR): calculated by using a standard formula, the APR shows the cost of a loan; expressed as a yearly interest rate, it includes the interest, points, mortgage insurance, and other fees associated with the loan

Application: the first step in the official loan approval process; this form is used to record important information about the potential borrower necessary to the underwriting process

Appraisal: a document that gives an estimate of a property's fair market value; an appraisal is generally required by a lender before loan approval to ensure that the mortgage loan amount is not more than the value of the property

Appraiser: a qualified individual who uses his or her experience and knowledge to prepare the appraisal estimate

ARM: Adjustable Rate Mortgage; a mortgage loan subject to changes in interest rates; when rates change, ARM monthly payments increase or decrease at intervals determined by the lender; the change in monthly payment amount, however, is usually subject to a cap

Ash Dump: An opening in the fireplace floor usually placed at the rear through which ashes are conveyed to the basement or outside.

Assessor: a government official who is responsible for determining the value of a property for the purpose of taxation

Assumable mortgage: a mortgage that can be transferred from a seller to a buyer; once the loan is assumed by the buyer, the seller is no longer responsible for repaying it; there may be a fee and/or a credit package involved in the transfer of an assumable mortgage

B

Balloon Mortgage: a mortgage that typically offers low rates for an initial period of time (usually 5, 7, or 10) years; after that time period elapses, the balance is due or is refinanced by the borrower

Bankruptcy: a federal law whereby a person's assets are turned over to a trustee and used to pay off outstanding debts; this usually occurs when someone owes more than they have the ability to repay

Base: A wood member carried around the walls of a room and touching the floor.

Base Mild: Moulding applied at top of base.

Base Shoe: Moulding applied at junction of base and floor.

Book Shelves: A group of shelves for storing books.

Boiler: A heating plant used to generate steam or hot water.

Borrower: a person who has been approved to receive a loan and is then obligated to repay it and any additional fees according to the loan terms

Bracing: Wood structural member installed to provide rigidity.

Bridal Registry: a program supported by the FHA that allows couples to open ("register" for) a bridal registry account into which family and friends can deposit gifts of cash; the funds in this account may then be used for a down payment on a house

Bridging: Wood members used to brace floor joists.

Building code: based on agreed upon safety standards within a specific area, a building code is a regulation that determines the design, construction, and materials used in building

Building Paper: Heavy water-proofed paper used over wall sheathing to provide insulation.

Budget: a detailed record of all income earned and spent during a specific period of time

C

Cap: a limit, such as that placed on an adjustable rate mortgage, on how much a monthly payment or interest rate can increase or decrease

Cash reserves: a cash amount sometimes required to be held in reserve in addition to the down payment and closing costs; the amount is determined by the lender

Cellar stair post: Post installed in cellar to support basement stair platform.

Cellar stair rail and post: Handrail for basement stairs and post to support handrail.

Certificate of title: a document provided by a qualified source (such as a title company) that shows the property legally belongs to the current owner; before the title is transferred at closing, it should be clear and free of all liens or other claims

Cleanout door: Cast iron door provided at bottom of chimeny for removing soot and debris in chimney stacks

Closing: also known as settlement, this is the time at which the property is formally sold and transferred from the seller to the buyer; it is at this time that the borrower takes on the loan obligation, pays all closing costs, and receives title from the seller

Closing costs: customary costs above and beyond the sale price of the property that must be paid to cover the transfer of ownership at closing; these costs generally vary by geographic location and are typically detailed to the borrower after submission of a loan application

Coal bin partition: Partition forming one side of coal bin.

Commission: an amount, usually a percentage of the property sales price, that is collected by a real estate professional as a fee for negotiating the transaction

Condominium: a form of ownership in which individuals purchase and own a unit of housing in a multi-unit complex; the owner also shares financial responsibility for common areas

Conventional loan: a private sector loan, one that is not guaranteed or insured by the U.S. government

Cooperative (Co-op): residents purchase stock in a cooperative corporation that owns a structure; each stockholder is then entitled to live in a specific unit of the structure and is responsible for paying a portion of the loan

Cornice: Wood moulding applied at junction of wall and ceiling. Occasionally used for hanging pictures.

Credit history: history of an individual's debt payment; lenders use this information to gauge a potential borrower's ability to repay a loan

Credit report: a record that lists all past and present debts and the timeliness of their repayment; it documents an individual's credit history

Credit bureau score: a number representing the possibility a borrower may default; it is based upon credit history and is used to determine ability to qualify for a mortgage loan

Cross bridging: Cross-bracing between floor joists to provide rigidity.

D

Damper control: Built in cast iron plate to regulate draft in fireplace.

Debt-to-income ratio: a comparison of gross income to housing and non-housing expenses; with the FHA, the monthly mortgage payment should be no more than 29% of monthly gross income (before taxes) and the mortgage payment combined with non-housing debts should not exceed 41% of income

Deed: the document that transfers ownership of a property

Deed-in-lieu: to avoid foreclosure ("in lieu" of foreclosure), a deed is given to the lender to fulfill the obligation to repay the debt; this process doesn't allow the borrower to remain in the house but helps avoid the costs, time, and effort associated with foreclosure

Default: the inability to pay monthly mortgage payments in a timely manner or to otherwise meet the mortgage terms

Delinquency: failure of a borrower to make timely mortgage payments under a loan agreement

Dining nook: A small area used for eating purposes.

Discount point: normally paid at closing and generally calculated to be equivalent to 1% of the total loan amount, discount points are paid to reduce the interest rate on a loan

Down payment: the portion of a home's purchase price that is paid in cash and is not part of the mortgage loan

E

Earnest money: money put down by a potential buyer to show that he or she is serious about purchasing the home; it becomes part of the down payment if the offer is accepted, is returned if the offer is rejected, or is forfeited if the buyer pulls out of the deal

Easing: A ramp in stair handrail.

EEM: Energy Efficient Mortgage; an FHA program that helps homebuyers save money on utility bills by enabling them to finance the cost of adding energy efficiency features to a new or existing home as part of the home purchase

Equity: an owner's financial interest in a property; calculated by subtracting the amount still owed on the mortgage loan(s)from the fair market value of the property

Escrow account: a separate account into which the lender puts a portion of each monthly mortgage payment; an escrow account provides the funds needed for such expenses as property taxes, homeowner's insurance, mortgage insurance, etc.

F

Face string and face mold: An exposed moulded wood member supporting stairs and stair railing.

Fair Housing Act: a law that prohibits discrimination in all facets of the home buying process on the basis of race, color, national origin, religion, sex, familial status, or disability

Fair market value: the hypothetical price that a willing buyer and seller will agree upon when they are acting freely, carefully, and with complete knowledge of the situation

Fannie Mae: Federal National Mortgage Association (FNMA); a federally-chartered enterprise owned by private stockholders that purchases residential mortgages and converts them into securities for sale to investors; by purchasing mortgages, Fannie Mae supplies funds that lenders may loan to potential homebuyers

FHA: Federal Housing Administration; established in 1934 to advance home-ownership opportunities for all Americans; assists homebuyers by providing mortgage insurance to lenders to cover most losses that may occur when a borrower defaults; this encourages lenders to make loans to borrowers who might not qualify for conventional mortgages

Finish floor: Final covering on floor, wood, linoleum, and carpet.

Finish floor 1 inch *x* 2 inch strips: Applied, over wood joists deadening felt, and diagonal sub-floor, before finish flooring is installed.

First floor joists: Wood structural members supporting first floor.

Fixed-rate mortgage: a mortgage with payments that remain the same throughout the life of the loan because the interest rate and other terms are fixed and do not change

Flood insurance: insurance that protects homeowners against losses from a flood; if a home is located in a flood plain, the lender will require flood insurance before approving a loan

Foreclosure: a legal process in which mortgaged property is sold to pay the loan of the defaulting borrower

Foundation wall: Masonry wall below ground supporting building.

Freddie Mac: Federal Home Loan Mortgage Corporation (FHLM); a federally-chartered corporation that purchases residential mortgages, securitizes them, and sells them to investors; this provides lenders with funds for new homebuyers

Furring strips: Wood strips nailed on masonry walls to which lath and plaster are applied.

G

Ginnie Mae: Government National Mortgage Association (GNMA); a government-owned corporation overseen by the U.S. Department of Housing and Urban Development, Ginnie Mae pools FHA-insured and VA-guaranteed loans to back securities for private investment; as with Fannie Mae and Freddie Mac, the investment income provides funding that may then be lent to eligible borrowers by lenders

Girder: A heavy wood or steel structural member supporting joists, beams, partitions or other structural members.

Girder post: Also called column. A post supporting a girder.

Good faith estimate: an estimate of all closing fees including pre-paid and escrow items as well as lender charges; must be given to the borrower within three days after submission of a loan application

H

Hearth: The floor of a fireplace.

HELP: Homebuyer Education Learning Program; an educational program from the FHA that counsels people about the home buying process; HELP covers topics like budgeting, finding a home, getting a loan, and home maintenance; in most cases, completion of the program may entitle the homebuyer to a reduced initial FHA mortgage insurance premium—from 2.25% to 1.75% of the home purchase price

Home inspection: an examination of the structure and mechanical systems to determine a home's safety; makes the potential homebuyer aware of any repairs that may be needed

Home warranty: offers protection for mechanical systems and attached appliances against unexpected repairs not covered by homeowner's insurance; coverage extends over a specific time period and does not cover the home's structure

Homeowner's insurance: an insurance policy that combines protection against damage to a dwelling and its contents with protection against claims of negligence or inappropriate action that result in someone's injury or property damage

Housing counseling agency: provides counseling and assistance to individuals on a variety of issues, including loan default, fair housing, and home buying

HUD: the U.S. Department of Housing and Urban Development; established in 1965, HUD works to create a decent home and suitable living environment for all Americans; it does this by addressing housing needs, improving and developing American communities, and enforcing fair housing laws

HUD-1 statement: also known as the 'settlement sheet," it itemizes all closing costs; must be given to the borrower at or before closing

HVAC: Heating, Ventilation and Air Conditioning; a home's heating and cooling system

I

Index: a measurement used by lenders to determine changes to the interest rate charged on an adjustable rate mortgage

Inflation: the number of dollars in circulation exceeds the amount of goods and services available for purchase; inflation results in a decrease in the dollar's value

Inside studs: Upright member of wood partition to which lath and plaster are applied.

Insulation: A heat retarding material applied in outside walls, top-floor ceiling or in roof to prevent passage of heat or cold in or out of building.

Interest: a fee charged for the use of money

Interest rate: the amount of interest charged on a monthly loan payment; usually expressed as a percentage

Interior doors and trim: Doors and. Finishing mouldings around door opening on inside of building

Interior window trim: Finishing mouldings used around window opening on inside of building.

Insurance: protection against a specific loss over a period of time that is secured by the payment of a regularly scheduled premium

J

Judgment: a legal decision; when requiring debt repayment, a judgment may include a property lien that secures the creditor's claim by providing a collateral source

L

Lease purchase: assists low-to moderate-income homebuyers in purchasing a home by allowing them to lease a home with an option to buy; the rent payment is made up of the monthly rental payment plus an additional amount that is credited to an account for use as a down payment

Lien: a legal claim against property that must be satisfied when the property is sold

Loan: money borrowed that is usually repaid with interest

Loan fraud: purposely giving incorrect information on a loan application in order to better qualify for a loan; may result in civil liability or criminal penalties

Loan-to-value (LTV) ratio: a percentage calculated by dividing the amount borrowed by the price or appraised value of the home to be purchased; the higher the LTV, the less cash a borrower is required to pay as down payment

Lock-in: since interest rates can change frequently, many lenders offer an interest rate lock-in that guarantees a specific interest rate if the loan is closed within a specific time

Lookouts: Horizontal wood members nailed to exterior wall upright and to roof rafters to provide extensions of roof beyond wall line.

Loss mitigation: a process to avoid foreclosure; the lender tries to help a borrower who has been unable to make loan payments and is in danger of defaulting on his or her loan

M

Main stair treads and risers: Tread-horizontal member which is stepped on. Riser-vertical member supporting the tread.

Mantle, shelf and trim: Finished wood covering around fire-place opening.

Margin: an amount the lender adds to an index to determine the interest rate on an adjustable rate mortgage

Mortgage: a lien on the property that secures the promise to repay a loan

Mortgage banker: a company that originates loans and resells them to secondary mortgage lenders like Fannie Mae or Freddie Mac

Mortgage broker: a firm that originates and processes loans for a number of lenders

Mortgage insurance: a policy that protects lenders against some or most of the losses that can occur when a borrower defaults on a mortgage loan; mortgage insurance is required primarily for borrowers with a down payment of less than 20% of the home's purchase price

Mortgage insurance premium (MIP): a monthly payment—usually part of the mortgage payment—paid by a borrower for mortgage insurance

Mortgage modification: a loss mitigation option that allows a borrower to refinance and/or extend the term of the mortgage loan and thus reduce the monthly payments

Mud sill: The lowest sill of a house.

O

Offer: indication by a potential buyer of a willingness to purchase a home at a specific price; generally put forth in writing

Origination: the process of preparing, submitting, and evaluating a loan application; generally includes a credit check, verification of employment, and a property appraisal

Origination fee: the charge for originating a loan; is usually calculated in the form of points and paid at closing

P

Partial claim: a loss mitigation option offered by the FHA that allows a borrower, with help from a lender, to get an interest-free loan from HUD to bring their mortgage payments up to date

Picture mold: Wood moulding applied at junction of wall and ceiling. Occasionally used for hanging pictures.

PITI: Principal, Interest, Taxes, and Insurance—the four elements of a monthly mortgage payment; payments of principal and interest go directly towards repaying the loan while the portion that covers taxes and insurance (homeowner's and mortgage, if applicable) goes into an escrow account to cover the fees when they are due

Plaster: A pasty material hardening on drying, used for coating walls, ceilings and partitions.

Plaster arch: An opening with a curved head formed in plaster.

Plaster arch brackets: Wood pattern cut to form curve of plaster arch, and to which lath and plaster are applied.

Plaster base: Also called lath; a wood, metal or gypsum material, nailed to wall and ceilings and. to which plaster is applied.

Plates (inside studs): Horizontal wood members nailed at bottom and top of partition uprights.

Plates (outside studs) : Horizontal wood members bolted to foundation wall and to which exterior wall uprights are nailed.

PMI: Private Mortgage Insurance; privately owned companies that offer standard and special affordable mortgage insurance programs for qualified borrowers with down payments of less than 20% of a purchase price

Porch frieze: Horizontal finishing member above porch columns and extending to roof boards.

Porch soffit: Underside of porch frieze.

Post base blocks (precast cement): Foundation for girder post.

Pre-approve: lender commits to lend to a potential borrower; commitment remains as long as the borrower still meets the qualification requirements at the time of purchase

Pre-foreclosure sale: allows a defaulting borrower to sell the mortgaged property to satisfy the loan and avoid foreclosure

Pre-qualify: a lender informally determines the maximum amount an individual is eligible to borrow

Premium: an amount paid on a regular schedule by a policyholder that maintains insurance coverage

Prepayment: payment of the mortgage loan before the scheduled due date; may be subject to a prepayment penalty

Principal: the amount borrowed from a lender; doesn't include interest or additional fees

R

Radon: a radioactive gas found in some homes that, if occurring in strong enough concentrations, can cause health problems

Rails and balusters: Handrails and vertical members of stair railing.

Real estate agent: an individual who is licensed to negotiate and arrange real estate sales; works for a real estate broker

REALTOR®: a real estate agent or broker who is a member of the NATIONAL ASSOCIATION OF REALTORS® and its local and state associations

Refinancing: paying off one loan by obtaining another; refinancing is generally done to secure better loan terms (like a lower interest rate)

Rehabilitation mortgage: a mortgage that covers the costs of rehabilitating (repairing or improving) a property; some rehabilitation mortgages—like the FHA's 203(k)—allow a borrower to roll the costs of rehabilitation and home purchase into one mortgage loan

RESPA: Real Estate Settlement Procedures Act; a law protecting consumers from abuses during the residential real estate purchase and loan process by requiring lenders to disclose all settlement costs, practices, and relationships

S

Second floor joists: Structural members supporting second floor.

Settlement: another name for closing

Special Forbearance: a loss mitigation option where the lender arranges a revised repayment plan for the borrower that may include a temporary reduction or suspension of monthly loan payments

Stair carriage: A wood member to which the treads and risers of a stairway are nailed.

Stair partition casing: A finished wood member used at junction of stair railing and partition.

Stair landing newel: Wood post into which stair railing abuts.

Starting newel: Wood post at start of wood railing of ascending stairway.

Starting tread and riser: The first step of an ascending stairway.

Sub-floor (diagonal): Floor which is laid in a diagonal fashion over the floor joists.

Subordinate: to place in a rank of lesser importance or to make one claim secondary to another

Survey: a property diagram that indicates legal boundaries, easements, encroachments, rights of way, improvement locations, etc.

Sweat equity: using labor to build or improve a property as part of the down payment

T

Termite shield: A metal protective shield applied on top of the foundation wall to prevent subterranean termites from attacking the structural wood members supporting the building.

Title I: an FHA-insured loan that allows a borrower to make non-luxury improvements (like renovations or repairs) to their home; Title I loans less than $7,500 don't require a property lien

Title insurance: insurance that protects the lender against any claims that arise from arguments about ownership of the property; also available for homebuyers

Title search: a check of public records to be sure that the seller is the recognized owner of the real estate and that there are no unsettled liens or other claims against the property

Truth-in-Lending: a federal law obligating a lender to give full written disclosure of all fees, terms, and conditions associated with the loan

Two-step mortgage: a type of adjustable rate mortgage that has one interest rate for a predetermined initial period and then adjusts to another rate that lasts for the term of the loan

U

Underwriting: the process of analyzing a loan application to determine the amount of risk involved in making the loan; it includes a review of the potential borrower's credit history and a judgment of the property value

V

VA: Department of Veterans Affairs: a federal agency which guarantees loans made to veterans; similar to mortgage insurance, a loan guarantee protects lenders against loss that may result from a borrower default

W

Wall stringer: Wood member secured to wall and which supports treads arid risers of stairway.

X

X-bracing: Frame bracing in a partition to provide rigidity.

0-595-27942-2

www.ingramcontent.com/pod-product-compliance
Lightning Source LLC
Chambersburg PA
CBHW030753180526
45163CB00003B/1008